CONTENTS

Ships in Focus Publications
Correspondence and editorial:
Roy Fenton
18 Durrington Avenue
London SW20 8NT
020 8879 3527
rfenton@rfenton.demon.co.uk

Orders and photographic:
John & Marion Clarkson
18 Franklands, Longton
Preston PR4 5PD
01772 612855
sales@shipsinfocus.co.uk
© 2003 Individual contributors, John
Clarkson and Roy Fenton.

Printed by Amadeus Press Ltd.,
Cleckheaton, Yorkshire.
Designed by Hugh Smallwood, John
Clarkson and Roy Fenton.
SHIPS IN FOCUS RECORD
ISBN 1 901703 70 3

SHIPS IN FOCUS
June

The short feature on Turner, Brightman in Record
great deal of interest, with an almost unprecedented and
follow up. The company was unusual amongst tramp ship owners
in providing insulated space for bringing meat from South
America. So rather than simply print all the feedback, it has been
decided to do more work on the company's history. The existence
of a detailed fleet list, and correspondence from one of the
founder's descendants, played their part in this decision. To those
who wrote to us about the company, we ask your patience: your
material has been valuable, it will be used and acknowledged, and
it has stimulated further research. If readers know of interesting
but obscure companies they would like us to feature in the same
way, please let us know, and we will oblige if we can.

In this issue we meet a long-standing request to include
photographs taken in an engine room. This is thanks to David
Aris, who is to be thanked for his patience in dealing with a non-
engineer editor. Colour reproduction seemed vital for this
feature, and hence we have enlarged our annual colour section to
24 pages. Readers are asked to bear with us when certain colour
features are separated from the articles they support: this is due to
the constraints of printing in 8- and 16-page sections.

In forthcoming issues we aim to make amends for
neglecting coastal shipping recently, beginning with a feature on
some early motor coasters.

As the last of the four issues that we notionally regard as
a volume of *Record*, this edition includes an index to *Records* 21
to 24. To accommodate this, and a little more, the size of this
issue has been increased by eight pages. This also gives an
opportunity to remind readers that they can get four issues of
Record bound by Ken Toft Bookbinders, Unit 4, Brassey Street
(off Laird Street), Birkenhead, CH41 8BY. The cost of binding
each volume is £16 plus £4 postage.
John Clarkson   Roy Fenton

SUBSCRIPTION RATES FOR RECORD

Subscribers make a saving on postage, and receive each *Record* just as
soon as it is published. They are also eligible for concessions on
newly-published *Ships in Focus* titles Readers can start their
subscription with *any* issue, and are welcome to backdate it to receive
previous issues.

	3 issues	4 issues
UK	£23	£32
Europe (airmail)	£25	£34
Rest of world (surface mail)	£25	£34
Rest of world (airmail)	£30	£40

Shaw, Savill's *Corinthic*. See pages 194 on. *[J. and M. Clarkson]*

Fleet in Focus
SHAW, SAVILL'S BIG ICs
Captain Edward Buckle and Roy Fenton

The passenger-cargo liner now seems an unlikely concept, mixing passengers - who demand intensive care when at sea, but are gone almost as soon as the ship docks - with cargo which takes a long time to load and discharge, during which time the accommodation is empty and the hotel staff barely employed. Yet, these ships were undeniably popular, both with passengers who found the atmosphere much less stuffy than on a big passenger ship, and with seafarers, some of whose fondest post-war memories are associated with them.

With fleet both ageing and much reduced by losses during the Second World War, Shaw, Savill gave high priority to replacement of their cargo ships. Early in 1945 they were allowed by the British Government to order two big refrigerated cargo liners from Cammell Laird and Harland and Wolff. Having considered Shaw, Savill's post-war needs at length, manager Basil Sanderson is said to have wanted to order two further vessels of this type, but fitted with accommodation for about 80 passengers. He was delighted to be told that it was not too late to change the design of the cargo ships. Two further ships were then ordered with very slight design changes.

The first of the quartet, *Corinthic,* had a serious fire in her hold whilst fitting out at Birkenhead in January 1947, but this did not delay her entry into service in April that year. *Athenic* followed from Belfast in August 1947. The second pair, Cammell Laird's *Ceramic* and Swan, Hunter's *Gothic,* made their maiden voyages a year later (details of launch and completion dates are in the accompanying fleet list).

They were twin-screw 15,000gt ships with 18,400 shaft horse power turbine machinery, the first steamers Shaw, Savill had ordered since 1928. There was surprise at this decision, as the company's *Dominion Monarch* had been the most powerful motorship in the world on delivery in 1939. Shaw, Savill were persuaded to revert to turbines by wartime advances in watertube boilers and reduction gearing.

Trading patterns and cargo
The ships originally tended to trade to both Australia and New Zealand via the Cape and Panama Canal. However, when the *Southern Cross* and *Northern Star* took up the regular round-the-world service the Big Ics, as they were known in the company, were placed permanently in the New Zealand trade. A typical voyage from London would be via Willemstad in Curacoa, Cristobal/Balboa, Panama Canal, Pitcairn Island and then Auckland and Lyttelton (outward) or Wellington/Port Chalmers. After completion of the outward discharge, loading would commence at the final discharge port and complete at either Auckland or Wellington via New Plymouth. Occasionally an extra loading port would be Timaru, Bluff or Opua in the Bay of Islands. The homeward voyage to London would be via Pitcairn Island, Balboa/Cristobal, and Willemstad in Curacao.

The ships had 532,000 cubic feet of refrigerated cargo capacity, with only 150,000 cubic feet for general cargo. Holds numbers 1 to 5 were completely refrigerated below the main deck level. General cargo spaces were the whole of number 6 hold plus numbers 3 and 4 hatch trunkways together with number 3 bridge space (see the diagram opposite, which represents the *Corinthic*). *Ceramic,* at least, had a bullion room and a special mail locker in the forecastle space.

On the homeward voyage number 2, 3, 4 and 5 lower holds would be full of butter and cheese. The locker spaces either side of the hatch squares in the upper and lower 'tween decks of number 2, 3, 4 and 5 would be full of cartons of meat and the centre sections such as number 1 hold and 'tween decks would be full of carcasses of lamb and mutton. The general spaces of numbers 6 and 3 and the trunkings end of the bridge space would contain casks of pelts, drums of tallow, milk powder, lactic casein and bales of wool.

The first of the Big Ics, *Corinthic,* is about to depart from a gloomy Liverpool on her maiden voyage, 12th December 1947. Built just across the Mersey in Birkenhead, she was the first Shaw, Savill ship built by Cammell Laird. When she was ordered in early 1945 the Ministry of Supply allocated what berths were available. Satisfaction with the *Corinthic* is suggested by the repeat order for *Ceramic,* and the contract for *Gothic's* pre-royal tour refit going to the Birkenhead yard. *[J. and M. Clarkson]*

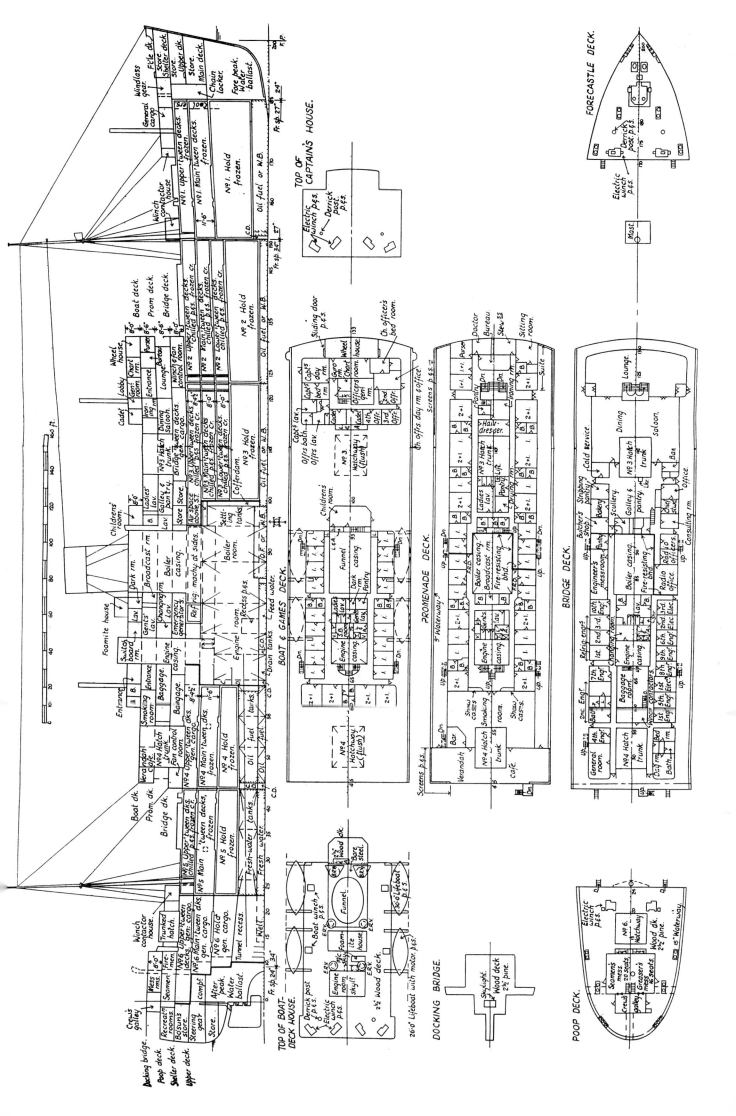

Passenger facilities

The ships carried 85 first class passengers in cabins on two decks. All cabins were fitted with bedsteads and had hot and cold running water. Single cabins had one large oblong window and the double cabins two. All windows were fitted with wooden inner louvres which enabled the windows to be down in the tropics and ensured privacy. Air conditioning was not fitted, but there were blower systems in all accommodation spaces providing cold air in summer and warm air in winter.

To port and starboard of the engine room casing on the boat deck were single cabins without facilities. Across the after end of this deck were three double cabins which could be converted to four berth. Baths had both fresh and salt water taps with fresh water shower overhead.

Forward on the starboard side of the passenger deck was the luxury suite with veneered panelling, and the only one other than the captain's and chief engineer's to have fitted carpets. The cabins port and starboard of the engine room casing from forward to the smoke room were a mixture of singles and doubles. Most had their own bathroom facilities, but adjacent to each bathroom was a single cabin with an adjoining door to the bathroom. This gave great flexibility when booking passengers as it allowed the option of a double or a single with facilities or, in the case of a family of three travelling, simple access from one cabin to the other.

Across the after end of the passenger deck was the large Verandah Café, and forward of that the smoke room and a small bar. At the forward end of the passenger deck was a hairdressing salon, a shop and the purser's office. The lounge at the forward end of the saloon deck also contained the library and writing room. This room was large enough to accommodate the passengers and senior officers when films had to be shown indoors because of inclement weather. Church services were also held there. The dining room seated all passengers and senior officers at one sitting. Each of the ships had paintings by distinguished artists in their smoke rooms and dining rooms. *Corinthic*, for instance, had paintings of wildfowl by Peter Scott.

Deck space was substantial, including the whole of the deck at the after end of the boat deck, and the large area between the deck officers' accommodation and the boat deck accommodation. These areas were covered with awnings in the tropics. There were also two large deck spaces either side of the passenger deck accommodation and there was a clear walk around the accommodation at saloon deck level. Here, canvas side screens were attached to the rails on the boat and passenger decks to reduce the wind flow. Entering and leaving port passengers were allowed on the monkey island above the deck officers' accommodation. The decks were wood throughout, even on the forecastle and poop decks.

Crew accommodation

The four ships always carried the most senior masters and chief engineers in the company, and one nearly always carried the commodore of the fleet. The master and chief engineer had their own suites, as did the chief officer and second engineer, although not on such an elaborate scale. The second officer's and junior second engineer's cabins were about the size of a far junior officer's cabin in Shaw, Savill cargo ships built about the same time. Despite this, they were very comfortable, and all had hot and cold water and plenty of drawer space under the bunk. The only snag was having to put the chair on the settee to open the drawers.

The petty officers' accommodation was in single cabins far larger than those of the officers with their own mess room and lounge. It was really comfortable, which was perhaps why petty officers stayed in the ships for years.

Catering ratings had large, two berth cabins with wooden bunk beds situated on the port side (see plans opposite). All had hot and cold water and a good-sized wardrobe and chest of drawers. There was a large mess room with a dartboard and table tennis table, and a comfortable lounge. Most of the catering staff returned trip after trip and the changes were only to the most junior ratings who had to move to progress their careers.

Surprisingly, accommodation for deck and engine room ratings was not up to the standard of that in contemporary Shaw, Savill cargo ships. These ratings were housed in the poop in twin cabins with metal bunk beds. There were small metal wardrobes and a large chest of wooden drawers. They shared a comfortable mess room and had a very large recreation room, across the after end of the deck. All cabins had hot and cold water. Despite the relatively poor accommodation, most ratings tended to return trip after trip. This could have been due to the regular sailings and the pleasant trip out to New Zealand and a four-week stay on the coast.

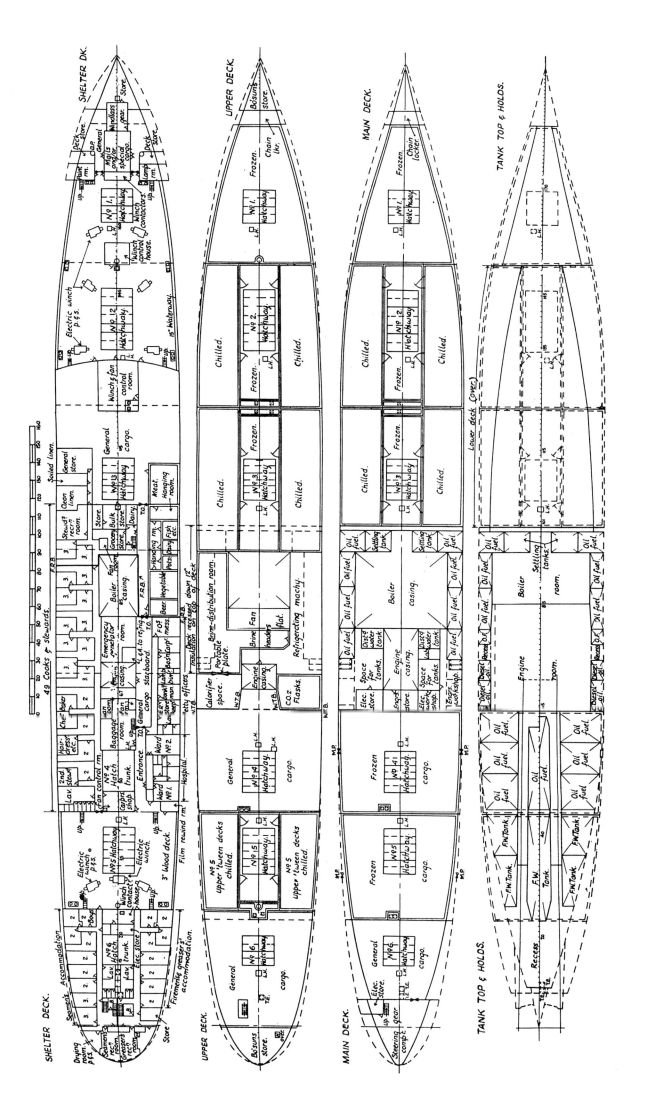

Ceramic, third of the class, in the New Zealand waters in which they were so popular. She lacks the white ribbon on her hull. *[J. and M. Clarkson]*

Social functions

On the New Zealand coast the four ships were very popular as venues for social functions. Dinner and luncheon parties were held on board by Rotary Clubs, the Meat Marketing Board, the Dairy Board, the Apple and Pear Board and the Master Mariners' Association. The size of the saloon was just right for their numbers and the accommodation was also available for those who had travelled into the port from far inland. The country farmers and officials from the cold stores in the heart of both North and South Island really appreciated the ships. The crew also enjoyed catering for them as there was a long period with no passengers between arriving on the coast and sailing again. The ships also had a regular flow of visiting school children from the small towns and villages of the interior. Some were seeing a ship for the first time and watched in awe as cartons of butter and cheeses, carcases of lamb and wool were loaded. They also liked the afternoon cream cakes and, on *Ceramic,* the hand-made chocolates specially prepared by the baker who was a very good confectioner.

Pitcairn islanders

All four ships were frequent callers at Pitcairn Island. Indeed, after many years of calling there the islanders more or less accepted the crews as their family. Edward can only recall one occasion when it was too rough for the islanders to launch their boats. On one visit *Ceramic's* stay was cut short due to the weather deteriorating. The stores and mail had been loaded into the boats but the islanders thought it too great a risk for the large drums of fuel oil to be discharged, as they had sufficient fuel until the next vessel called and did not want the boats damaged. The *Ceramic* departed at about lunchtime but by six o'clock in the evening she had not received the usual radio message that the islanders had returned safely so it was decided to return just in case there was a problem. Shortly after midnight, in mountainous seas as the ship approached the south of the island, a message was received that

they had just landed safely in Bounty Bay and were dragging the boats clear of the water.

In the 1950s the Pitcairn islanders travelled regular to nearby uninhabited islands, to Henderson for miro wood which was used for their carvings and to Oeno for pandanus leaves which were used for making baskets. Henderson was 105 miles east north east of Pitcairn and *Ceramic* would pick up their boats when on its homeward journey and drop them off close to a landing area. Here they would spend about four days fishing and cutting the timber they required and then sail home, which took 18 to 24 hours. On one occasion the islanders were taken to Oeno, a very low-lying atoll was about 70 miles west of Pitcairn. There was very little vegetation except for a few palm trees but pandanus grew well. The fishing was excellent and there were some unusual shells which were used for necklaces.

In the 1960s, as the numbers on the island dwindled and the women outnumbered the men, they became reluctant to travel to these two islands. The younger men did not like leaving the older ones in charge as there had become a large age difference.

When a new school building was taken out from New Zealand, it was shipped in sections. When discharged, instead of it being placed on two boats lashed together, the islanders requested that it was placed in the sea and, after discharging their mail, stores and fuel in the harbour, they returned to the open sea to tow the various sections ashore.

On another call a small caterpillar tractor was to be delivered which the islanders decided would be better dismantled to be taken ashore. *Ceramic's* engineers jumped into action and within a couple of hours had reduced it to what the islanders thought were manageable pieces. As the sections were dismantled they were marked so the islanders would be able to reassemble them. However, they neither had the tools or the knowledge and some months later a representative of the makers was taken out to rebuild the tractor.

Correspondence with readers (see for instance, George Robinson's letter on page 112 of *Record* 22) on the subject of altering photographs prompts the inclusion of the postcard above, produced by Shaw, Savill. Suspicion was aroused when one of the editors found in his collection another company postcard purporting to show the starboard side of *Gothic* which was, in fact, from the same negative but reversed: details of the sea and sky are identical. Looking closely, the names of the ships have been crudely added, and are far too prominent: the yellow paint the owners used did not stand out that well. Comparison of genuine photographs of the sisters show some small differences:

notably the aftermost of the openings alongside the accommodation at main deck level - in the *Gothic* this is square but in the *Ceramic* it is rounded, as it is in the two earlier ships. From this it is concluded that the above photograph shows *Ceramic,* but whether her port or starboard side is unclear.

Another suspicious feature is the Thornycroft funnel top, which looks too large and its louvres rather too well-defined to be true. Quite likely, this is an early photograph taken of *Ceramic* - perhaps on trials - before this feature was fitted, and which has been retouched. Clearly, photographs have been telling lies since long before the advent of the Apple

Mac and Adobe Photoshop!

Although many photographs of *Gothic* and *Ceramic* have been examined in preparing this article, none have been found which show them without the Thornycroft top; if any reader can provide an acceptable photograph, we will be pleased to reproduce it.

The photograph by John McRoberts of *Ceramic* at Liverpool reproduced below is dated 23rd August 1952. She is still without the pair of kingposts ahead of the funnel which can be seen in the other photographs of *Ceramic* in this feature. [Top: Shaw, Savill, Roy Fenton collection; below: J. and M. Clarkson]

Gothic and the royal tourists

Late in 1950 preparations began for a royal tour of the Commonwealth to take place in 1952, it being intended that the King George VI, Queen Elizabeth and Princess Margaret would take part. As the existing royal yacht *Victoria and Albert* was in no fit state for a long tour, and her replacement, *Britannia,* was not going to be ready in time, it was decided to use a cargo passenger ship. After the King had made a private visit to *Corinthic* whilst she was berthed in London during October 1950, the choice of one of this quartet was confirmed. It is said that *Ceramic* was originally chosen, but other sources maintain that the first choice was always to be the *Gothic,* newest of the four. *Gothic* received a new livery for her role as royal yacht, being repainted white early in 1951, but *Ceramic* was also repainted white as standby vessel.

The royal tour was subject to delay and then postponement due to the ill health and later the death of the King. *Gothic* was extensively prepared with royal apartments being fitted, much of the work being carried out by Cammell Laird at Birkenhead. In view of the King's poor health, it was decided that the then Princess Elizabeth and the Duke of Edinburgh would carry out the visit, and the *Gothic* left for Mombasa in Kenya where they were due to embark in February 1952. However, the King died before this could take place, and the tour was cancelled. *Gothic* then continued on her voyage to Sydney. On return to the UK she was partly reconverted for normal trading with a reduced passenger complement, but the royal apartments were sealed and left, although some furniture and fittings were removed.

The royal tour got underway late in 1953, by when Princess Elizabeth had become Queen. Further work on *Gothic* was done at Birkenhead, including air-conditioning of the royal apartments and the smoke room, and putting on board some of the furnishings from the *Victoria and Albert.* Her complement was massively increased, from the normal 124 to a total of 283. *Gothic's* merchant navy crew had grown to 168, the others made up of Royal Naval personnel, the Royal Yacht Band, newspaper correspondents, and many members of the royal household - the master recalling that there were 'secretaries to the secretaries'. In truth, many of them had little to do during the voyage, coming along because they were experts in ceremonial procedure. *Gothic* was also to carry a vice admiral, notwithstanding that she was at all times to have a naval escort.

It has been said that *Gothic* carried her regular crew, but the officers at least seem to have been hand-picked. Shaw, Savill's senior master, David Aitchison, was appointed from the *Dominion Monarch.* Some of the other preparations seem over elaborate: the cook was sent to the kitchens of both the Savoy Hotel and one of the royal households for experience. Another odd, but much more practical, decision was to carry full cargoes out and home. In fact, the *Gothic* was to have so much time off in Australia and New Zealand, when she functioned as little more than a royal baggage store, that discharge and loading of the cargo in no way interfered with the tour's schedule.

The Queen and Duke of Edinburgh flew to Jamaica, and *Gothic* with her escort (initially the cruiser HMS *Sheffield*) crossed the Atlantic to pick them up there. At first, it was decided that *Gothic* was to take station on the escort, which was in charge of navigation, but this as reversed when it was found the merchant service had the better navigators, perhaps not surprisingly as to Shaw, Savill officers a voyage through the Panama Canal and across the Pacific was routine.

During certain parts of the voyage a very tight schedule had to be maintained, and Captain Aitchison felt it a matter of honour that *Gothic* was absolutely punctual. This was not always easy: when one of her later escorts, HMNZS *Black Prince,* lost a man overboard in the Pacific, she and *Gothic* turned back to make a search, unsuccessfully as it turned out, and *Gothic* had to steam flat out at 18½ knots to regain schedule. This may have had unfortunate repercussions, as the spurt was blamed for damage which was later found to *Gothic's* high-pressure turbine. Captain Aitchison was mortified at the possibility of any bad publicity for his ship, and the damage was hushed up. Fortunately, *Gothic* could make good speed with one of her high-pressure turbines uncoupled, and her sister *Ceramic* gave up her turbine which was flown out from London to Sydney for fitting in *Gothic.* Only then, when personnel of Cockatoo Dockyard gave a hint to the press that something was amiss, did the incident receive any publicity, and by now, with the trouble sorted out, it had lost its sting.

Captain Aitchison was chosen for his seniority, but when writing his very readable account of the voyage, *Royal Standard, Red Ensign,* he was very candid about the occasions when he was in a flap. Some incidents seem, in retrospect, very trivial, like the generator breakdown whilst in port that might, at the worst, have deprived the Queen of a hot breakfast. But Captain Aitchison's responsibilities were by no means minor. For instance, during a royal sightseeing cruise which took *Gothic* inside the Great Barrier Reef he hardly left the bridge, despite having a senior pilot on board. Most frightening of all was the arrival off Cocos Island in the Indian Ocean, where the original plan of anchoring off this coral island proved impossible: the water was far too deep. With heavy surf breaking on the shore, the master with great trepidation took *Gothic* very close to the reef at the only sheltered spot from where he reckoned the royal party could be sent ashore safely by barge.

Looking back from almost half a century, and from a possibly more cynical age, the pomp and protocol insisted upon during the royal tour seem preposterous, and the adulation the royal party received excessive, although this was the first time a reigning monarch had visited New Zealand or Australia. However, the royal tour was judged a great success, and *Gothic* and her crew had played their part in it to perfection. Just before the Queen left *Gothic,* honours were distributed; the engineer in charge of the air conditioning being singled out for an award. Captain David Aitchison received a well-deserved knighthood. *Gothic* had made an excellent royal yacht.

Towards the end of her career, when her passenger accommodation had been turned over mainly to the use of the crew, *Gothic* suffered a tragic fire. It was detected in the smoke room on 1st August 1968, when she was heading across the Pacific in a force 8 gale. Fanned by the gale, the fire quickly engulfed most of the passenger accommodation, trapping several people. Before the fire was got under control there were seven deaths, including a family of four travelling as supernumeraries. *Gothic's* bridge and wireless equipment were completely destroyed,

Above: *Gothic* still in her royal yacht livery in June 1954. This photograph shows why *Gothic* needed to be painted no fewer than four times during the royal tour. Indeed, keeping the hull white became an obsession during the voyage and it was touched up at most ports, sometimes under arclights. A photograph of *Gothic* in the Mersey, reproduced on page 72 of our photograph album 'Feilden's Mersey', shows her hull in much worse condition.

It has been suggested that *Gothic's* slightly older sister, *Ceramic,* was originally selected as the royal yacht, and that in preparation she received some improvements. Most notably, these included the fitting of a Thornycroft top to the funnel to reduce the soot fallout on the upper decks when tubes were being blown, and also to carry the smoke well clear. A similar top was then fitted to *Gothic*

There were a number of differences between the first and second pairs of Big Ics. The first two were fitted with a stem post at the bow and the later two ships had a soft-nose bow, which account for the distinctive shapes of the two bows. *Athenic* and *Corinthic* had conventional cowl ventilators ahead of the funnel: *Ceramic* and *Gothic* had mushroom vents. See also page 232.

Below: *Gothic* in her normal hull livery. She has now been fitted with the extra pair of kingposts and derricks immediately ahead of the funnel which distinguished the latter two ships of this class. [Both: J. and M. Clarkson]

and her return to New Zealand - navigated by a chart and compass from one of her lifeboats - was something of an epic. Repairs estimated at £300,000 were not considered worthwhile given her age, but she was patched up for one more round voyage, being sold to shipbreakers in Kaohsiung in 1969.

The end of an era

During the 1960s the cargo passenger liner had come to the end of its days on all but a very few very specialised routes. Shaw, Savill, themselves abandoned it in the 1950s for the principle of the 'pure' passenger liner with the *Southern Cross,* and her belated consort *Northern Star.* The inescapable logic was that, whilst the ship was delivering its cargo round Australia and New Zealand, its passenger accommodation was empty, and the stewards and catering staff that served it largely idle. Far better not to carry cargo, and to make another voyage as soon as passengers and their baggage had been unloaded. Once the 1962-built *Northern Star* had settled into her routine with the *Southern Cross,* it became uneconomical to carry passengers on all four of the cargo passenger ships, and it was decided to accept no more bookings for three of the ships from 1965. *Ceramic,* however, remained a passenger ship until she arrived in London on 3rd July 1968 with 37 passengers from New Zealand. Unlike the *Corinthic* and *Gothic,* her passenger accommodation was not converted for use by the crew, but was stripped out and sealed.

It is ironic that Shaw, Savill, having abandoned the cargo passenger ship, should have had wished on them three such ships from Royal Mail Lines, made redundant from the River Plate service. Shaw, Savill never really wanted the *Akaroa, Aranda* and *Arawa,* and not surprisingly their careers on the Australasian service were short before they were sold and gutted to become car carriers.

It is sobering to note how few of the cargo passenger ships made redundant in the 1970s found their way to other owners, as did most contemporary pure cargo ships. Certainly, all four Big Ics went straight from Shaw, Savill ownership to the breakers. In the case of *Athenic,* and probably others, the crew who took her to the breakers felt they were delivering a ship in first class condition, before her time.

In July 1965, when no longer carrying passengers, *Athenic* had her accommodation cut back and lost one set of lifeboats, changes which had a disproportionate effect on her appearance, as the view above shows. *Ceramic,* below, did not have her accommodation cut back after she ceased carrying passengers in 1968. See also page 232. *[Both: J. and M. Clarkson]:*

Personal memories

Let the last words of this narrative be those of Captain Edward Buckle, who served extensively on *Ceramic*.

'To see one of the Big Ics leaving Wellington or Auckland fully loaded and newly painted was a wonderful sight. One voyage, I was relieving the chief officer on the *Northern Star,* and we happened to be in Wellington with the *Ceramic*. Standing on the deck watching her leave on her homeward trek a passenger turned to me and said 'Doesn't she look bloody lovely!' I think he noticed a tear in my eye as he also passed a complimentary remark about the *Northern Star.*

When I left at the end of the *Ceramic's* last passenger voyage, I was informed that it was to be one of the two big ones - *Northern Star* or *Southern Cross* - for me until I was promoted to master. The expression on my face must have related something to our Marine Manager. He asked me what I didn't like about the big ones seeing I had been on them from time to time. I realised I had to come up with an appropriate answer. After some thought I replied, "Going from the *Ceramic* to the *Northern Star* or the *Southern Cross* is like going from Harrods to Woolworths". I think he received the message because shortly after my leave I was appointed to *Akaroa,* previously Royal Mail's *Amazon.*

Ceramic and her sisters were excellent sea ships, well built and very comfortable in all sea states. They were seldom delayed due to heavy weather and rarely received heavy weather damage. All were happy ships and the crew were just like one happy family and that is perhaps why they were efficiently run, so well liked by the passengers, and so successful as cargo carriers.'

Ships' details and dates

Tonnages are from *Lloyd's Register* 1949.

CORINTHIC   1947-1969   Twin screw
O.N. 187909 15,682g 9,097n 559.8 x 71.2 x 40.7 feet
Six steam turbines by Cammell, Laird and Co. Ltd., Birkenhead geared to two shafts; 17 knots.
30.5.1946: Launched by Cammell, Laird and Co. Ltd., Birkenhead (Yard No. 1175) for Shaw, Savill and Albion Line Ltd., London as CORINTHIC.
4.1947: Completed.

12.4.1947: Left on maiden voyage from Liverpool to New Zealand.
23.10.1969: Arrived at Kaohsiung to be broken up by China Steel Corporation.
11.1969: Work began.

ATHENIC   1947-1969   Twin screw
O.N. 167927 15,187g 8,767n 560.4 x 71.2 x 40.7 feet
Six steam turbines by Harland and Wolff Ltd., Belfast geared to two shafts; 17 knots.
26.11.1946: Launched by Harland and Wolff Ltd., Belfast (Yard No. 1326) for Shaw, Savill and Albion Co. Ltd., London as ATHENIC.
7.1947: Completed.
1.8.1947: Left on maiden voyage from London to New Zealand.
7.1965: Converted to cargo only by Swan, Hunter and Wigham Richardson Ltd., Wallsend-on-Tyne.
25.10.1969: Arrived at Kaohsiung to be broken up by Hwa Zon Iron and Steel Co.
5.11.1969: Work began.

CERAMIC   1948-1972   Twin screw
O.N.182344   15,896g 9,162n 560.9 x 72.2 x 40.7 feet
Six steam turbines by Cammell, Laird and Co. Ltd., Birkenhead geared to two shafts; 17 knots.
30.12.1947: Launched by Cammell, Laird and Co. Ltd., Birkenhead (Yard No. 1185) for Shaw, Savill and Albion Co. Ltd., London as CERAMIC.
10.1948: Completed.
13.6.1972: Passed Antwerp bound for Temse to be broken up by J. Boel et Fils.
25.9.1972: Work began.

GOTHIC 1948-1969 Twin screw
O.N. 182351 15,902g 9,150n 561.0 x 72.2 x 40.7 feet
Six steam turbines by Wallsend Slipway Co. Ltd., Wallsend-on-Tyne geared to two shafts; 17 knots.
12.12.1947: Launched by Swan, Hunter and Wigham Richardson Ltd., Wallsend-on-Tyne (Yard No. 1759) for Shaw, Savill and Albion Co. Ltd., London as GOTHIC.
12.1948: Completed.
13.8.1969: Arrived at Kaohsiung for breaking up by Hwa Zon Iron and Steel Co.
5.11.1969: Work began.

A classic Basil Feilden shot of *Corinthic,* from a negative which, it seems, has failed to survive. *[World Ship Photo Library collection]*

THE IRON LADIES Part 2
John Harrison

Machinery

Most of the ore carriers were powered by diesel engines, the Doxford type being the commonest. The first two ships, the *Gleddoch* and the *Ormsary,* were fitted with triple-expansion steam reciprocating engines. Seven of the Port Talbot type ships had twin geared diesel engines, the *Gerore,* the *La Colina,* the *Oredian,* the *Orelia,* the *Oreosa,* the *Orepton* and the *Philippe LD.* This type of engine was lighter and more compact, while gearing permitted the choice of optimal propeller revolutions. One engine could be stopped at sea for maintenance whilst still keeping a reasonable speed. This facility was particularly useful in view of the short time that the ships spent in port.

The ship with the most interesting engines, however, was the *Morar* which was fitted with free piston gas turbine engines. She was the first British ship and the first ocean-going ship to be built with free piston propulsion. She was jointly owned by the shipbuilding companies, Connells and Lithgows, and the shipping companies, Clarksons and Denholms, to be a floating testbed for what at that time was a new system of propulsion. The agreement for her construction included an indemnity which provided that the shipowners would be reimbursed by the shipbuilding companies for any additional running costs compared with her conventionally-powered sister ships. The main reason for choosing an ore carrier for this experiment was that, with comparatively long voyages and short turnaround times, an ore carrier would provide a more strenuous testing ground than a conventional cargo ship. Also, with more frequent returns to the United Kingdom, monitoring the effectiveness of her machinery was easier.

A number of advantages were claimed for the gas turbine, the principle ones being more compact machinery and savings in weight. The reduction in the size of the *Morar's* engine room provided additional cargo space and water ballast. Also, as the engine room casing was smaller, the size of poop house was reduced without reducing the crew accommodation. The weight of her machinery was 410 tons compared with 630 tons for her sister ship, the *Orecrest.* She was also able to carry 200 tons deadweight

of extra cargo compared with the *Orecrest.* It was reckoned that the capital cost of the machinery for larger gas turbine ships would eventually be less than that of comparable diesel machinery. In addition, the maintenance costs would be lower as gas turbines use smaller interchangeable units. When the *Morar* was being built it was considered that fuel costs would be less for gas turbine ships, particularly as she could burn boiler fuel. In practice this saving was not achieved, partly because no attempt was made to recirculate exhaust gas from the generators. Although more expensive to run than a comparative motor ship, her running costs were cheaper than an equivalent steam turbine vessel. The design of the *Morar's* engines did much to overcome the noise problems that earlier gas turbine units had experienced.

She was originally fitted with three free-piston generators and a gas turbine. As part of the development programme, however, her original gas turbine was replaced by four generators of modified design after a year. The reason for adding a fourth generator was to enable the ship to operate whilst a defective generator was repaired at sea.

The *Morar* proved to be so very unreliable that her charter was ended prematurely by mutual agreement after nine years. She was then sold and re-engined with a conventional diesel. In designing the vessel her builders had not taken full advantage of the opportunity that gas turbines offered of having a smaller engine room, so that a diesel could be installed at a later date, if required.

Being a somewhat experimental vessel, the *Morar's* design incorporated a number of other innovative features as well as her engines. Of particular interest were the use of rolling hatch covers of a type that had not previously been used on a British ship, the use of plastic piping in the crew's quarters and some glass fibre piping in the engine room and a new type of insulating material on her deck plating.

Careers

Ignoring what appear to have been paper transactions where ships were transferred from one subsidiary company to another for tax and other reasons, two ships changed

The gas-turbine driven *Morar* at North Shields on 2nd March 1967. *[J. and M. Clarkson]*

hands during their charter periods. Clyde Shipping's *Needles* was acquired by Denholms in 1960, becoming the *Wellpark*. After a brief foray into deep-sea shipping earlier in the nineteenth century, the Clyde Shipping Company owned only tugs and coasters, so possibly they felt that operating a much larger ship was not really in their interests. The Norwegian *Farland* became the *Gerland* in 1963, having been sold by I/S Farland to A/S Gerrards Rederi.

The elusive *Needles* at Barrow-in-Furness, 16th August 1958. *[Ian Harmsworth]*

Although several ships were involved in casualties during their charter periods, only in one instance was the damage so bad that the charter was curtailed. In August 1972 fire broke out on board the *Nordland* whilst at Rotterdam and as a result her charter was ended a year early. She was sold in her damaged state and subsequently rebuilt.

Initially the building programme was very successful. It resulted in considerable savings in the cost of ore shipments to Britain. Furthermore, the operation of these specialist ships was a more efficient process than the previous one of chartering ships for individual voyages or short periods, thus ensuring more regular supplies of ore to Britain's steelworks. The initial success of the scheme is emphasised when it is realised that 10 or 15-year charter agreements were entered into for what was then a revolutionary type of ship initially when the ships themselves were only at design stage.

As the programme continued, however, it became apparent that, with the benefit of hindsight, the Corporation had perhaps made the mistake of putting all its eggs in one basket. Three reasons can be given for this. Firstly, the ships were unsuitable for the carriage of return cargoes. Secondly, the number of ore carriers built represented a fixed capacity of ore transport and at times of recession BISC was overprovided with shipping. Thirdly, the ships themselves became outdated in terms of the needs of the trade for which they were designed.

When they were built the prime need was seen as being for ships that would bring ore to the United Kingdom in the most efficient way. They were designed to carry the maximum weight of ore within the constraint of the hull dimensions and also the maximum weight of ballast on return voyages. All other considerations were sacrificed to these objectives as the need to bring ore to the country was the main and most urgent consideration. Thus no thought was given to the carriage of return cargoes and, when possible cargoes were investigated at a later stage, no suitable ones could be found. For instance, their holds were too small to carry coal and the ships were not fitted with cargo gear to handle steel products and, in any event, it was difficult to co-ordinate the export of steel products with the import of iron ore. The Lyle ships were designed so they could carry grain as well as ore, but as far as is known no other ships were designed to take alternative cargoes. The St. Denis Shipping Company ships were

adapted to carry grain in the early 1970s (see below), but were not particularly successful in this role.

The lack of versatility in cargo-carrying capacity exacerbated the difficulties that occurred in times of recession in the steel industry. As the ships could not be redeployed for other uses, they had to be laid up. At one point in the early 1960s when the completion of several ore carriers within a short period resulting in additional capacity coming on stream coincided with a slump in the steel industry, a number were laid up.

The shipping requirements of the ore trade changed during the period of the charters. As the number of steelworks declined ore imports were required at a smaller number of ports, thus making it sensible to use larger ships. Furthermore, the ports themselves had been adapted to take larger ships. For instance, in the 1960s a new harbour was built at Port Talbot so the small size of the Port Talbot class was no longer needed. In addition, Immingham and Redcar on the Tees had been developed to take larger vessels. These changes were, of course, accompanied by an increase in the size of bulk carriers generally and ore carriers in particular, thus making it sensible for the British Steel Corporation, as BISC had then become, to use larger ships.

The culmination of these trends was that British Steel reverted to a policy of chartering ships for individual voyages or short periods. In the immediate post-war years there had been few purpose-designed ore carriers, but by the 1970s not only ore carriers but also bulk carriers and OBOs designed to carry ore were commonplace. Thus the Corporation could operate more flexibly in the charter market without risk to ore supplies. As the long-term charters expired they were not renewed on a regular basis, although some of the ships were chartered back for single voyages or for short periods, particularly those that passed to the Pothitos group.

With two exceptions all the ships were sold by their original owners when their charters expired or a short time afterwards. Only the *Oregis* which was converted to a diving support and oil well maintenance ship remained in the ownership of the Houlder Group, until scrapped at the end of 1982. The *Essex* was converted to the bulk chemical tanker *Essi Anne* at the expiry of her charter period by I/S Essex. Six ships were broken up at the expiry of their charters.

An amusing story relates to the sale of the *Sagamore* to Societa Riunita di Navigazione SrL. In March 1959 the then captain of the ship acquired a pedigree Siamese kitten, Princess Tao-Tai and this cat passed to the subsequent ship's master. In 1975 the ship was put up for sale and the owners proposed to have the cat, now fifteen and a half years old, put down. The story was, however, leaked to the press and featured in most national newspapers and on the television and radio. As a consequence, an outcry from animal welfare societies ensued. The only way for the owners to avoid bad publicity was to include a clause in the sale of the ship that the cat was allowed to remain on the ship and be kept in the manner she was accustomed for the rest of her life!

One particular group acquired a number of the vessels, the Greek Pothitos group. The ships that passed to this group generally received names commencing with *Dapo* or *Evpo* or girls' names. The *Dapo* prefix was made up from a combination of the names of the two partners in the company, N. Davaris and E. Pothitos, and the *Evpo* prefix from a combination of Evangelos Pothitos' first name and surname. As well as ships with the *Dapo* or *Evpo* prefixes, the *Michalis, Katina, Mary, Susie, Ady, Hadiotis* and *Filia* (originally *Dukesgarth, Dunadd, Duncraig, Dunkyle, Joya McCance, Redcar* and *Sir Andrew Duncan* respectively) belonged to this group.

To be continued

FLEET LIST (part two)

J. AND J. DENHOLM (MANAGEMENT) LTD., GLASGOW

Details of *Naess Trader,* in which Denholms had a 40% stake, will appear under Naess Denholm and Co. Ltd. Previously Clyde Shipping's *Needles, Wellpark* was acquired by Denholm Line Steamers Ltd. part way through her charter. For details of *Dunblane* which was acquired by St. Andrews Shipping Co. Ltd. after the expiry of her charter, refer to Bolton Steam Shipping's *Redcar* in *Record 23.*

H. Clarkson and Co. Ltd., London (J. and J. Denholm (Management) Ltd., Glasgow, managers).

CLARKAVON (PT) 1957-1972
O.N. 187726 6,860g 3,117n 9,300d 425'6" x 57'4" x 25'4¼"
3-cyl. 2SCSA Doxford-type oil engine by North Eastern Marine Engineering Co. Ltd., Wallsend-on-Tyne; 600 x 2,320, 2,600 BHP, 11.25 knots.
7.11.1957: Launched by Short Brothers Ltd., Sunderland (Yard No. 529) for H. Clarkson and Co. Ltd., London (J. and J. Denholm (Management) Ltd., Glasgow, managers) as CLARKAVON.
2.1958: Completed.
13.11.1972: Arrived Faslane for demolition by Shipbreaking Industries Ltd.

CLARKEDEN (PT) 1958-1973
O.N. 300204 6,861g 3,119n 9,200d 425'6" x 57'4" x 25'4¼"
3-cyl. 2SCSA Doxford-type oil engine by William Doxford and Sons (Engineering) Ltd., Sunderland; 600 x 2,320, 2,600 BHP, 11.25 knots.
7.3.1958: Launched by Short Brothers Ltd., Sunderland (Yard No. 530) for H. Clarkson and Co. Ltd., London (J. and J. Denholm (Management) Ltd., Glasgow, managers) as CLARKEDEN.
7.1958: Completed.
1973: Sold to Phaedon Shipping Co. SA, Panama (Stavros A. Daifos, Piraeus, Greece) and renamed PHAEDON under the Greek flag.
1974: Sold to Prekookeanska Plovidba, Bar, Yugoslavia and renamed BERANE.
30.4.1982: Arrived at Split for demolition by Brodospas.

Clarkson's two ore carriers: *Clarkavon* (above) and *Clarkeden* (below). *[J. and M. Clarkson (no relation); Malcolm Cranfield]*

St. Andrews Shipping Co. Ltd. (J. and J. Denholm (Management) Ltd., managers), Glasgow

DUNADD 1955-1973
O.N. 185773 10,682g 5,391n 14,000d
505'0" x 69'0" x 27'6"
4-cyl. 2SCSA Doxford-type oil engine by David Rowan and Co. Ltd., Glasgow; 670 x 2,320, 3,717 BHP, 12 knots.
7.10.1955: Launched by Lithgows Ltd., Port Glasgow (Yard No. 1099) for St. Andrews Shipping Co. Ltd. (J. and J. Denholm (Management) Ltd., Glasgow, managers as DUNADD.
12.1955: Completed.
1973: Sold for £250,000 to Compania Susie SA, Panama (Leonidas N. Pothas, Piraeus, Greece) and renamed KATINA under the Greek flag.
16.7.1975: Laid up at Piraeus
1975: Managers became Dapo SA (N.A. Davaris), Piraeus, Greece.
1977: Sold to CWS International SA, Panama (Alta Shipping Ltd., Piraeus, Greece) and renamed ALFA CEMENTA.
1978: Reported converted for use as a cement silo and storage facility in Saudi Arabia.
1980: Deleted from 'Lloyd's Register'.

Dunadd was the site of the ancient capital of Dalrinda from which the Celtic Kingdom sprang.

DUNCRAIG 1956-1973
O.N. 185784 10,687g 5,398n 14,300d
505'1" x 69'0" x 27'6"
4-cyl. 2SCSA Doxford-type oil engine by David Rowan and Co. Ltd., Glasgow; 670 x 2,320 4,500 BHP, 11.5 knots.
4.12.1956: Launched by Lithgows Ltd., Port Glasgow (Yard No. 1100) for St. Andrews Shipping Co. Ltd. (J. and J. Denholm (Management) Ltd.), Glasgow as DUNCRAIG.
3.1957: Completed.
1967: Owners became British Steam Shipping Co. Ltd., Cardiff.
1973: Sold to Compania Reginald SA, Panama (Leonidas N. Pothas, Piraeus, Greece) and renamed MARY under the Greek flag.
11.6.1975: Laid up at Piraeus.
1975: Managers became Dapo SA (N.A. Davaris), Piraeus, Greece.
1979: Beneficial owners E. Pothitos, E. Koutsofios and others, Piraeus and renamed EVPO MARY.
4.9.1982: Arrived Gadani Beach for demolition by Paruma International.

This ship was named in honour of Sir John Craig, honorary president and former chairman of Colville's Steel Company. Duncraig is a village in Ross and Cromarty.

DUNKYLE 1957-1973
O.N. 185790 10,687g 5,398n 14,300d
505'1" x 69'0" x 28'11¼"
4-cyl. 2SCSA Doxford-type oil engines by David Rowan and Co. Ltd., Glasgow; 670 x 2,320, 4,500 BHP, 11.5 knots.
12.11.1957: Launched by Lithgows Ltd., Port Glasgow (Yard No. 1101) for St. Andrews Shipping Co. Ltd. (J. and J. Denholm (Management) Ltd., managers), Glasgow as DUNKYLE.
12.1957: Completed.
1973: Sold to Compania Susie SA, Panama (Leonidas N. Pothas, Piraeus, Greece) for £150,000 and renamed SUSIE under the Greek flag.
1975: Managers became Dapo SA (N.A. Davaris), Piraeus, Greece.
23.11.1979: Arrived at San Esteban for demolition by Desguales Aviles.

This vessel was named after Mr D.H. Kyle, managing director of BISC (Ore) Ltd.and she was launched by his wife.

Dunadd on trials. *[Roy Fenton collection]*

Duncraig off the Alfred entrance to Birkenhead docks. *[Bernard McCall]*

Dunkyle. [J. and M. Clarkson]

SIR ANDREW DUNCAN   1958-1973

O.N. 300487   10,687g 5,398n 14,300d
505'1" x 69'0" x 28'11¼
4-cyl. 2SCSA Doxford-type oil engines by
David Rowan and Co. Ltd., Glasgow; 670
x 2,320, 5,150 IHP,11.5 knots.
25.2.1958: Launched by Lithgows Ltd.,
Port Glasgow (Yard No. 1103) for St.
Andrews Shipping Co. Ltd. (J. and J.
Denholm (Management) Ltd., managers),
Glasgow as SIR ANDREW DUNCAN.
5.1958: Completed.
1967: Owners became British Steam
Shipping Co. Ltd., Cardiff.
1973: Sold to Compania Filia SA, Panama
(Leonidas N. Pothas, Piraeus, Greece) and
renamed FILIA under the Greek flag.
1975: Managers became Dapo SA (N.A.
Davaris), Piraeus, Greece.
5.4.1979: Arrived in tow at Abidjan Roads.
In position 04.15 north by 02.47 west
during a voyage from Rostock to Lagos
with a cargo of cement, her engine room
had flooded, damaging her machinery, and
a crack had developed in her hull.
Declared a constructive total loss and sold
to Eckhardt & Co. KG on behalf of Spanish
shipbreakers.
1.12.1979: Left Abidjan in tow for Bilbao
where she arrived on 31.12.1979. She was
subsequently broken up at Santander by
Recuperaciones Submarinas SA.

Until his death in 1952 Sir Andrew Duncan
was chairman of the British Iron and Steel
Federation and he was a former Minister of
Supply and President of the Board of
Trade.

In 1973 *Dunblane* (ex *Redcar*), *Duncraig*
and *Sir Andrew Duncan* were sold in a
£1,000,000 block deal to the Pothitos
Group, other members of the group
subsequently joining them.

**Scottish Ore Carriers Ltd. (J. and J.
Denholm   (Management)   Ltd.,
managers), Glasgow.**

ARISAIG (PT)   1957-1962

O.N. 185788 6,872g 3,115n 9,000d 427'
0" x 57'3" x 25'4½";
3 cyl. 2SCSA Doxford-type oil engine by
David Rowan and Co. Ltd., Glasgow, 600 x
2,320, 2,500 BHP, 10.5 knots.
3.6.1957: Launched by Lithgows Ltd., Port
Glasgow (Yard No. 1110) for Scottish Ore
Carriers Ltd. (J. and J. Denholm
(Management) Ltd., managers), Glasgow
as ARISAIG.
9.1957: Completed.
1.5.1972: Arrived Faslane for demolition
by Shipbreaking Industries Ltd.

The *Arisaig* was named after a village
situated between Fort William and Mallaig.

CRAIGALLIAN (PT) 1959-1974

O.N. 300498   7,088g 3,434n 9,703d
427'0" x 57'2" x 25'6½"
3-cyl. 2SCSA Doxford-type oil engines by
Barclay Curle and Co. Ltd., Glasgow; 600
x 2,320, 2,500 BHP, 11 knots.
2.10.1959: Launched by Charles Connell
and Co. Ltd., Scotstoun (Yard No. 491) for

Sir Andrew Duncan off Clydebank, July 1972. *[J.K. Byass]*

Arisaig arriving at Port Talbot. *[J. and M. Clarkson]*

Craigallian approaching Eastham Locks, August 1971. *[J. and M. Clarkson]*

Scottish Ore Carriers Ltd. (J. and J.
Denholm (Management) Ltd., managers),
Glasgow as CRAIGALLIAN.
12.1959: Completed.
1974: Sold to Zapata Offshore Services
Ltd., London (Denholm Ship Management
Ltd., Glasgow, managers).

14.5.1975: Laid up at Moji.
5.6.1976: Having been sold to Nissho-Iwai
Co. Ltd. left in tow for Inchon, South Korea
for demolition by Sang Yong Trading Co.
Ltd.
11.8.1976: Work began.

CRINAN (PT) **1960-1974**
O.N. 302197 7,086g 3,431n 9,703d 427'3"
x 57'2" x 25'6¹/₂"
3-cyl. 2SCSA Doxford-type oil engine by
Barclay, Curle and Co. Ltd., Glasgow; 600
x 2,320, 2,500 BHP, 11 knots.
17.2.1960: Launched by Charles Connell
and Co. Ltd., Scotstoun (Yard No. 492) for
Scottish Ore Carriers Ltd. (J. and J.
Denholm (Management) Ltd., managers),
Glasgow as CRINAN.
4.1960: Completed.
1974: Sold to K/S A/S Geir (Th. F. Fekete,
manager), Tonsberg, Norway and renamed
KLAR.
1976: Sold to Luzon Stevedoring
Corporation, Manila, Philippines and
renamed LSCO TAWI TAWI.
1977: Converted to ore/oil carrier, gross
tonnage now 5,324.

1982: Owners became Philippine National
Oil Co. (PNOC) Tankers Corporation,
Manila and renamed PNOC TAWI TAWI.
1983: Owners became PNOC Coal
Corporation, Manila and renamed LAKE
TAAL. Subsequently converted to bulk
carrier, gross tonnage now 5,324.
17.7.1987: Sold by auction to Wallem
Philippines Shipping Inc. for resale for
demolition.
12.8.1987: Went aground at Batangas
during Typhoon Betty.
9.1987: Refloated.
21.10.1987: Arrived Kaohsiung for
demolition by An Hsiung Iron and Steel Co.
2.11.1987: Work began.

The Crinan Canal links Loch Fyne to the
Sound of Jura.

GLEDDOCH (PT) **1952-1970**
O.N. 185765 6,859g 3,180n 9,150d 427'0"
x 57'3" x 25' 3¹/₂"
T. 3-cyl, 26", 44" and 76" x 48" by Rankin
and Blackmore Ltd., Greenock; 3,000 IHP;
11 knots.
18.12.1952: Launched by Lithgows Ltd.,
Port Glasgow (Yard No. 1094) for Scottish
Ore Carriers Ltd. (J. and J. Denholm
(Management) Ltd., managers), Glasgow as
GLEDDOCH.
5.1953: Completed.
1970: Sold to Claudio Marinzulich
(Agenzia Marittima Duodo e Co.,
managers), Venice, Italy and renamed
ALDO CERCONI.
1977: Sold to Esperide Societa di
Navigazione SpA, Milan, Italy.
1978: Sold to Itta Ruggeri for demolition at
Vado Ligure.

The ship was named after the Langbank
home of the Lithgow family (see *Ormsary*
below).

Above: *Crinan* in September 1961. Below: *Gleddoch*. [Both: J. and M. Clarkson]

Above: Morar at Port Talbot in April 1959, and below re-engined and equipped with some butch-looking cargo gear, as the German *Arnis*.

[J. and M. Clarkson; Author's collection]

MORAR (PT) 1958-1967

O.N. 300492   6,990g 2,699n   9,250d
427'0" x 57'3" x 25'3½"

Three free-piston gas generators, 2SA, each 1-cyl. 340 x 550 and one Pescara-type gas turbine geared to screw shaft by British Polar Engines Ltd., Glasgow and Rankin and Blackmore Ltd., Greenock; 11 knots.

23.4.1958: Launched by Lithgows Ltd., Port Glasgow (Yard No. 1113) for Scottish Ore Carriers Ltd. (J. and J. Denholm (Management) Ltd., managers), Glasgow as MORAR.

1.1959: Completed.

3.1961: Engines replaced (details as original engines except for an additional gas generator).

4.1967: Sold to Reederei Barthold Ritchers, Hamburg, Germany and renamed CLARI.

10.1967: Re-engined with 9-cyl. 2SCSA oil engine by Werkspoor NV, Amsterdam; 450 x 700.

1969: Sold to Seeredeerei Arnis H.P. Vith and Co. KG, Flensburg, West Germany and renamed ARNIS.

1972: Owners became Arnis Shipping Co. Ltd., Nicosia, Cyprus (Beereederungs-Alliance Flensburg GmbH, Flensburg, Germany).

11.1973: Sold to PT Indonesian National Bulk Carrier, Djakarta, Indonesia.

1974: Renamed MAHONI.

26.9.1979: Ran aground on the west coast of Taiwan in position 23.33 north by 119.42 east whilst carrying a cargo of cement. Holed and engine room flooded. Subsequently declared a total loss.

6.1980: Refloated and sold for breaking up to Chai Tai Steel and Enterprise, Kaohsiung.

17.10.1980: Work began.

Morar is a district in the West Highlands of Scotland and also the name of a village.

Ormsary entering Birkenhead docks in June 1956. *[J. and M. Clarkson]*

ORMSARY (PT) 1952-1969

O.N. 185761 6,859g 3,180n 9,150d 427'0" x 57'2" x 25'3½"

T. 3-cyl. 26", 44", 76" x 48" by Rankin and Blackmore Ltd., Greenock; 3,000 IHP; 11.5 knots.

26.8.1952: Launched by Lithgows Ltd., Port Glasgow (Yard No. 1092) for Scottish Ore Carriers Ltd. (J. and J. Denholm (Management) Ltd), Glasgow as ORMSARY.

1.1953: Completed.

3.11.1969: Arrived at Bilbao for demolition by Hierros Ardes.

The ship was named after the Argyll home of the Lithgow family (See *Gleddoch* above).

FURNESS WITHY AND CO. LTD., LONDON

EDENMORE 1957-1973
O.N. 187762 10,792g 5,686n 15,876d
505'1" x 67'3" x 29'0¼"
4-cyl. 2SCSA Doxford-type oil engine by David Rowan and Co. Ltd., Glasgow; 670 x 2,320, 4,000 BHP, 12 knots.
24.12.1957: Launched by Blythswood Shipbuilding Co. Ltd., Glasgow (Yard No. 122) for Furness Withy and Co. Ltd., London as EDENMORE.
4.1958: Completed.
12.1973: Owners became Pacific Maritime Services Ltd., London.
17.3.1975: Sold to Attlich Co. Inc., Panama (Gino Gardella, Genoa, Italy) and renamed WELCOME.
1976: Sold to Cala Pira SpA di Navigazione, Cagliai, Italy and renamed DUGLASIA.
15.9.1983: Arrived at Savona en route to Vado for demolition by G. Riccardi.
10.1983: Reported lying at Vado.
1.1984: Demolition commenced.

SAGAMORE 1957-1973
O.N. 187699 10,792g 5,686n 15,884d
505'1" x 67'3" x 29'0"
4-cyl. 2SCSA Doxford-type oil engine by David Rowan and Co. Ltd., Glasgow; 670 x 2,320, 4,000 BHP, 12 knots.
12.9.1957: Launched by Blythswood Shipbuilding Co. Ltd., Glasgow (Yard No. 121) for Furness Withy and Co. Ltd., London as EDENMORE.
12.1957: Completed.
12.1973: Owners became Pacific Maritime Services Ltd., London.
27.2.1975: Sold to Navale Cala di Volpe SpA, Cagliai, Italy and renamed CAPITAN ALBERTO.
1985: Sold to Societa Riuniti di Navigazione SpA, Cagliari, Italy.
1989: Sold to Sivilla Maritime Inc., Monrovia, Liberia (Stylianos Markakis, Piraeus, Greece) and renamed TANIA under the St. Vincent flag.
13.6.1992: Arrived Alang for demolition by Gopi Chand and Co.
12.7.1992: Work began.

Above: Edenmore in May 1973. Below: Sagamore. [Both J. and M. Clarkson]

GIBBS AND CO. (SHIP MANAGEMENT) LTD., NEWPORT
Welsh Ore Carriers Ltd. (Gibbs and Co. (Ship Management) Ltd., managers), Newport

WELSH HERALD (L) 1963-1976
O.N. 303643 19,543g 9,859n 27,740d
615'0" x 84'6" x 32'0¾"
6-cyl. 2SCSA Gotaverken-type oil engine by North Eastern Marine Engineering Co. Ltd., Newcastle-upon-Tyne; 760 x 1,500, 7,500 BHP, 13 knots.
6.2.1963: Launched by Austin and Pickersgill Ltd., Sunderland (Yard No. 824) for Welsh Ore Carriers Ltd. (Gibbs and Co. (Ship Management) Ltd., managers), Newport as WELSH HERALD.
4.1963: Completed.
7.1976: Sold to Astramar Compania Argentina di Navegacion SAC, Buenos Aires, Argentina and renamed ASTRAPATRICIA.
11.1976 to 2.1977: Converted to lightening vessel by Hapag-Lloyd, Bremerhaven.
1990: Sold to Ultraocean S.A. (Oceanmarine S.A.), Buenos Aires.
1992: Registered in Panama.
30.11.1993: Arrived at Chittagong Roads for demolition.
About 18.12.1993: Moved on to Chittagong to be broken up by Z.N. Enterprise.

Welsh Herald at South Shields, 5th October 1963. [George Scott; J. and M. Clarkson]

HOULDER BROTHERS AND CO. LTD., LONDON
Ore Carriers Ltd. (Houlder Brothers and Co. Ltd., managers), London

For details of the *Ravensworth* owned for a short time by this company see under R.S. Dalgliesh Ltd. Furness Withy's *Edenmore* and *Sagamore* were managed by Houlders from 1971.

JOYA McCANCE 1960-1975
O.N. 301246   11,871g 4,813n 16,830d
513'11" x 69'1" x 28'10¼"
4-cyl. 2SCSA Doxford-type oil engine by Central Marine Engineering Works, Hartlepool; 670 x 2,320, 5,500 BHP, 13 knots.
11.7.1960: Launched by William Gray and Co. Ltd., Hartlepool (Yard No. 1307) for Ore Carriers Ltd. (Houlder Brothers and Co. Ltd., managers), London as JOYA McCANCE.
10.1960: Completed.
6.10.1961: Collided off Brunsbuttelkoog with the Dutch coaster THEA (500/1957, NV Carebeka) which subsequently sank.
13.7.1966: Owners became South American Saint Line Ltd. (Houlder Brothers and Co. Ltd., managers), London and renamed ST MARGARET.
1970: Owners became Ore Carriers Ltd.
1975: Sold to Independent Carriers Inc., Panama (Del Bene Ultramar, SACIF, Buenos Aires, Argentina).
1978: Sold to Hadiotis Shipping Co. SA, Panama (E. Pothitos, E. Koutsofios and others, Piraeus, Greece) and renamed HADIOTIS.
12.7.1985: Damaged her intermediate tailshaft between Smalkalden and Puerto Adaz on the River Orinoco and subsequently declared a constructive total loss. Laid up in the river prior to being sold to Terminales Puerto Adaz for scrapping. Subsequently resold to Maritime Ordaz for use as a barge on the River Orinoco.
1.5.1989: Arrived in tow at Aliaga for demolition by Cukurova Celik Endustrisi AS. She had been sold to Turkish shipbreakers through St. Vincent flag interests.
13.5.1989: Beached prior to demolition.

MABEL WARWICK 1960-1975
O.N. 301070   11,632g 4,679n 16,550d
506'0" x 69'1" x 28'11½"
4-cyl. 2SCSA Doxford-type oil engine by Central Marine Engineering Works, Hartlepool; 670 x 2,320, 5,500 BHP, 13 knots.
14.2.1960: Launched by William Gray and Co. Ltd., Hartlepool (Yard No. 1301) for Ore Carriers Ltd. (Houlder Brothers and Co. Ltd., managers), London as MABEL WARWICK.
6.1960: Completed.
24.10.1975: Sold to Celika Navigation Co. Ltd., Limassol, Cyprus (Roussos Brothers, Piraeus, Greece) and renamed NIKOLAOS MALEFAKIS.
1980: Sold to Rubini Shipping Co. EPE (Const. Tsamopoulos), Piraeus, Greece and renamed RUBINI.
12.7.1982: Arrived at Piraeus with machinery damage sustained on a voyage from Caen. Declared a constructive total loss and sold to Ploioscrap Ltd for demolition at Eleusis.
8.6.1983: Work began.

Joya McCance (top) was named after the wife of Sir Andrew McCance, a director of the owners and Chairman of Colvilles, who launched the ship. She was renamed *St Margaret* (middle) to keep alive the naming system of the South American Saint Line whose title Houlders acquired when the company ceased trading and sold all its ships. This freed the name *Joya McCance* for a new tanker. *Mabel Warwick* (bottom) was named after the lady who launched it, the wife of S.C. Warwick, at that time the chairman of Houlder Brothers and Ore Carriers Ltd. *[A. Duncan; Bernard McCall; A. Duncan]*

OREDIAN (PT) 1955-1971

O.N. 186258 6,859g 3,219n 9,258d 427'0" x 57'3" x 25'6"

Two 5-cyl. 2SCSA oil engines with hydraulic coupling and SR gearing to screw shaft by Central Marine Engineering Works, Hartlepool; 500 x 700, 3,652 BHP, 12.5 knots.

22.4.1955: Launched by William Gray and Co. Ltd., Hartlepool (Yard No. 1269) for Ore Carriers Ltd. (Houlder Brothers and Co. Ltd., managers), London as OREDIAN.

7.1955: Completed.

4.1971: Sold to Allied Finance SA (D.J. Chandris), Piraeus, Greece and renamed OREDIAN STAR.

1973: Sold to Marifoam Shipping Co. Ltd., Nicosia, Cyprus (D.J. Chandris, Piraeus, Greece) and renamed MARICHANCE.

27.2.1974: Delivered to China National Metals and Minerals Import and Export Corporation, Hsinkang, China for breaking up.

OREGIS (PT) 1955-1972

O.N. 186303 6,858g 3,009n 9,050d 427'0" x 57'3" x 25'6¼"

5-cyl. 2SCSA Doxford-type oil engines by Hawthorn Leslie and Co. Ltd., Newcastle-upon-Tyne; 560 x 1,680, 3,400 BHP, 12.5 knots.

25.7.1955: Launched by William Gray and Co. Ltd., Hartlepool (Yard No. 1272) for Ore Carriers Ltd. (Houlder Brothers and Co. Ltd., managers), London as OREGIS.

11.1955: Completed.

26.12.1969: Grounded on a sandbank off the entrance to Workington. Refloated two days later, having closed the entrance to the port.

24.6.1972: Owners became Vallum Shipping Co. Ltd.

6.4.1973: Arrived on River Tyne for conversion to a diving support ship and oil well maintenance vessel by Swan Hunter Ship Repairers Ltd., Wallsend-on-Tyne. Gross tonnage changed to 6,448 tons.

7.5.1973: Owners became Ore Carriers Ltd.

10.3.1974: Ran aground off Tynemouth when engines failed when leaving the Tyne following completion of her conversion.

8.4.1974: Refloated.

8.1974: Renamed HTS COUPLER 1.

23.10.1975: Owners became Houlder Offshore Ltd. and renamed OREGIS.

25.11.1982: Left Tyne in tow having been sold to Spanish shipbreakers.

3.12.1982: Arrived Vigo to be broken up by Miguel Martins Pereira.

2.1983: Work began.

ORELIA (PT) 1953-1971

O.N. 186007 6,858g 3,268n 8,975d 427'0" x 57'2" x 25'6"

Two 5-cyl. 2SCSA oil engines with hydraulic coupling and SR gearing to single screw shaft by Central Marine Engineering Works, Hartlepool; 500 x 700, 3,652 BHP, 12.5 knots.

9.10.1953: Launched by William Gray and Co. Ltd., Hartlepool (Yard No. 1262) for Ore Carriers Ltd. (Houlder Brothers and Co. Ltd., managers), London as ORELIA.

3.1954: Completed.

1971: Sold to Allied Finance SA (D.J. Chandris), Piraeus, Greece and renamed ORELIA STAR.

1973: Sold to Oreliastar Shipping Co. Ltd., Nicosia, Cyprus (D.J. Chandris, Piraeus, Greece) and renamed MARISUERTA.

4.5.1974: Delivered to China National Metals and Minerals Import and Export Corporation, Hsinkang, China for breaking up.

From top to bottom: *Oredian, Oregis* in the Manchester Ship Canal, probably bound for the Irlam Steel Works and again at Tynemouth 16th March 1974, and *Orelia.* Their names were chosen by Sir John Houlder as basically pleasant-sounding words with the prefix *Ore.* [*Fotoflite incorporating Skyfotos; Ken Cunnington; J. and M. Clarkson; Roy Fenton collection*].

OREMINA (PT) 1956-1974

O.N. 187391 6,858g 3,010n 9,235d 427'0" x 57'3" x 25'6¼"

5-cyl. 2SCSA Doxford-type oil engines by Hawthorn Leslie and Co. Ltd., Newcastle-upon-Tyne; 560 x 1,680, 3,400 BHP, 12 knots.

28.2.1956: Launched by William Gray and Co. Ltd., Hartlepool (Yard No. 1273) for Ore Carriers Ltd. (Houlder Brothers and Co. Ltd., managers), London as OREMINA.

5.1956: Completed.

1972: Owners became Vallum Shipping Co. Ltd.

1974: Sold to Navale Cala di Volpe SpA, Cagliari, Italy (Landi e C., Genoa, Italy) and renamed GENERALE FEDERICO.

8.3.1985: Arrived at Savona for demolition by Italian shipbreakers.

16.4.1986: Demolition commenced at Vado Ligure by G. Riccardi.

OREOSA (PT) 1954-1971

O.N. 186064 6,856g 3,267n 8,975d 427'0" x 57'2" x 26'0";

Two 5-cyl. 2SCSA oil engines with hydraulic coupling and SR gearing to single screw shaft by Central Marine Engineering Works, Hartlepool; 500 x 700, 3,400 BHP, 12.5 knots.

4.2.1954: Launched by William Gray and Co. Ltd., Hartlepool (Yard No. 1263) for Ore Carriers Ltd. (Houlder Brothers and Co. Ltd., managers), London as OREOSA.

5.1954: Completed.

4.1971: Sold to Allied Finance SA (D.J. Chandris), Piraeus, Greece and renamed OREOSA STAR.

1973: Sold to Mariluck Maritime Co. Ltd., Nicosia, Cyprus (D.J. Chandris, Piraeus, Greece) and renamed MARILUCK.

1974: Sold to Preekookeananska Plovidba, Bar, Yugoslavia and renamed PODGORICA.

1988: Sold to Dabinovic International SA, Panama (Dabinovic SA, Geneva, Switzerland) and renamed ALMADEN under the St. Vincent flag.

4.1989: Demolition began by Arya Steel at Alang.

OREPTON (PT) 1954-1971

O.N. 186206 6,859g 3,219n 9,258d 427'0" x 57'2" x 25'6";

Two 5-cyl. 2SCSA oil engines with hydraulic coupling and SR gearing to single screw shaft by Central Marine Engineering Works, Hartlepool; 500 x 700, 3,400 BHP, 12.5 knots.

10.12.1954: Launched by William Gray and Co. Ltd., Hartlepool (Yard No. 1268) for Ore Carriers Ltd. (Houlder Brothers and Co. Ltd., managers), London as OREPTON.

3.1955: Completed.

4.1971: Sold to Allied Finance SA (D.J. Chandris), Piraeus, Greece and renamed OREPTON STAR.

1973: Sold to Orepton Shipping Co. Ltd., Nicosia, Cyprus (D.J. Chandris, Piraeus, Greece) and renamed MARITIHI.

16.5.1974: Delivered to China National Metals and Minerals Import and Export Corporation, Hsinkang, China for breaking up.

It is understood that when the *Oredian, Orelia, Oreosa* and *Orepton* were sold to the Chandris Group company, they were merely transferred from lay up berths at Falmouth to lay up berths at Piraeus and were not traded before being resold.

Top to bottom: Oremina at Eastham, Orepton in April 1958, and Oreosa in Sven Salen colours. [J. and M. Clarkson; Fotoflite incorporating Skyfotos]

LYLE SHIPPING CO. LTD., GLASGOW

CAPE FRANKLIN   1959-1974
O.N. 301392   11,815g 6,212n 15,500d
524'6" x 70'0" x 27'3"
2SCSA 5-cyl. Burmeister and Wain-type
oil engine by J. and G. Kincaid and Co.
Ltd., Greenock; 620 x 1,400, 4,500 BHP,
11.5 knots.
9.3.1959: Launched by Lithgows Ltd., Port
Glasgow (Yard No. 1127) for Lyle
Shipping Co. Ltd., Glasgow as CAPE
FRANKLIN.
3.1959: Completed.
1974: Sold to Gino Gardella, Genoa, Italy
and renamed VITTORIA GARDELLA.
1988: Sold to Sylianos Markakis, Piraeus,
Greece and renamed VITO under the St.
Vincent flag.
15.7.1988: Arrived Alang for demolition
by Alang Shipbreakers Pvt. Ltd..

Cape Franklin in September 1967. *[J. and M. Clarkson]*

CAPE HOWE (L)   1962-1978
O.N. 304148   19,032g 11,567n 27,941d
608'0" x 80'0" x 32'4¼"
2SCSA 5-cyl. Burmeister and Wain-type oil
engine by J. and G. Kincaid and Co. Ltd.,
Greenock; 620 x 1,400, 6,410 BHP, 12 knots.
31.5.1962: Launched by Lithgows Ltd.,
Port Glasgow (Yard No1137) for Lyle
Shipping Co. Ltd., Glasgow as CAPE
HOWE.
11.1962: Completed.
1978: Sold to Albion Maritime Inc.,
Monrovia, Liberia (Gulf Shipping Lines
Ltd., London) and renamed AL TAWWAB
under the Singapore flag.
28.1.1984: Left Osaka for Beilun,
Zhejiang, China to be broken up, arriving
about 5.2.1984.

CAPE NELSON 1961-1976
O.N. 301446   12,351g 6,185n 16,450d
524.6" x 69'1" x 27.6"
2SCSA 5-cyl. Burmeister and Wain-type oil
engine by J. and G. Kincaid and Co. Ltd.,
Greenock; 620 x 1,400, 4,500 BHP, 12 knots.
15.2.1961: Launched by Lithgows Ltd.,
Port Glasgow (Yard No 1128) for Lyle
Shipping Co. Ltd., Glasgow as CAPE
NELSON.
4.1961: Completed.
1976: Sold to Compania Sydenham SA,
Panama (E. Pothitos, E. Koutsofios and
others, Piraeus, Greece) and renamed
DAPO WAVE under the Greek flag.
1978: Renamed EVPO WAVE.
27.4.1981: Collided two miles off
Demerara with the motor fishing vessel
ARENQUE (705/1966; Cuban
Government) which subsequently sank.
1982: Sold to Gurunegala Shipping Co. Ltd.,
Colombo, Sri Lanka (E. Pothitos, Piraeus,
Greece) and renamed CEYLAN WAVE.
11.3.1985: Ran aground in the River
Orinoco off Paramibo whilst bound for
Puerto Ordaz.
20.3.1985: Refloated.
25.1.1989: Arrived at Chaguaramas after
water had entered her hatches whilst
outward bound from Mantanzas,
Venezuela. Declared a total loss.
28.6.1989: Arrived Mamonal for demolition
by S.I.P.S.A. Columbia.
20.7.1989: Work began.
To be continued.

Cape Howe [J. and M. Clarkson]

Cape Nelson. [J. and M. Clarkson]

IN A LIBERTY SHIP ENGINE ROOM

David Aris

During the Second World War a total of 2,710 Liberty-type ships were built in 18 US shipyards. Their design was based on a vessel constructed by the shipyard of J.L. Thompson and Sons at North Sands, Sunderland. In addition to the Liberties, there were 60 Ocean type vessels built in the USA, and 354 Fort, Park, Victory and Canadian class ships built in Canada. Add to these the nine Empire ships built by Thompson for the UK government, and a total of 3,133 identical hulls were built, the largest class of ocean-going vessels ever constructed.

Today there are just two Liberty ships left, operational but non-commercial; the *John W. Brown* in Baltimore and the *Jeremiah O'Brien* in San Francisco. The latter had her keel laid at the New England Shipbuilding Yard in Portland, Maine on 6th May 1943 and was delivered on 30th June. She made seven round voyages during the war, along with 11 trips to the Normandy beaches from D-day plus 3. Following the war she was laid up for 33 years until 1979 when she began to be restored by volunteers. In 1994 she returned to England and France in connection with the fiftieth anniversary of the Normandy landings.

The accompanying colour photographs of the machinery, accommodation and wheel house were taken by the author, the UK representative for the owners of *Jeremiah O'Brien*, the National Liberty Ship Memorial, during the return voyage from France to San Francisco in 1994.

Below. Jeremiah O'Brien arriving in the Medway following its visit to Normandy in 1994. The sight of a Liberty steaming into a British port once again after so many years was something very special. *[Roy Fenton]*

Above. The operating side of an engine awaiting installation in a Liberty. This was built by that prolific engine builder, Joshua Hendy Iron Works of Sunnyvale, near San Jose, California. *[Author's collection]*

Left. Looking aft from the boiler space through the triple-expansion steam engine, designed by North Eastern Marine Engineering Co. Ltd., Wallsend-on-Tyne and built by the General Machinery Corporation, Hamilton, Ohio. Note the original, rather poor, lighting and paintwork. The cylinder diameters are 24½, 37, and 70 inches, and the stroke 48 inches. Total weight of the engine is 121 tons. To the left, painted with aluminium heat-resisting paint, is the front casing of the starboard boiler. Overhead are insulated steam lines to various pieces of auxiliary machinery. On the front column of the engine is a vertical shaft with a large brass horizontal hand-wheel at the bottom, the main hand-operated throttle for controlling engine speed. In front of this is a steel lever and another vertical shaft, the hand throttle connected to a butterfly valve in the steam line, which is used to prevent the engine racing when, in bad weather, the propellor could come out of the water. Governors were not fitted when the Liberties were built, although some owners fitted them post-war.

Below. The middle platform of the main engine, taken with the engine running at 66 rpm - hence the blurred crosshead. In the centre can be seen the Stephenson link motion valve gear operating the low-pressure cylinder slide valve. Part of the linkage from the crosshead to the revolution counter can be seen, a brass bracket fastened to the column in the foreground. This transmits the motion to a revolution counter at the bottom platform

Above left. The main engine, showing the top of the cylinders, the piston valve cover for the high-pressure cylinder, the high-pressure cylinder cover and intermediate-pressure cylinder slide valve cover. The silver-painted insulated valve at the bottom is the main throttle valve, and is supplied by the two silver-painted superheated steam pipes from port and starboard boilers. The seven black hand-wheels control valves admitting steam to various other ship services, including whistle, heating, and deck steam.

Opposite top right. The high-pressure crank, bottom end bearing and connecting rod. These bearings are completely hand lubricated. The cast-iron bedplate bearing pockets which carry the main bearings are square in section. If a bearing wipes and needs replacement, it means hanging up all connecting rods and valve gear, then lifting the complete crankshaft, which weighs 17.8 tons. Fortunately, the engine is very reliable if well cared for and it is very rarely necessary to carry out this operation. Modern practice is to have the bearing housings machined half round, so that removal of the shells can be done with the crankshaft *in situ.*

Opposite bottom left. A view through the main engine looking aft. The crankpin is shrunk-fitted into the crank web but also has a round dowel pin fitted, a long-outdated practice. Immediately behind the handrail are the eccentrics for the high-pressure cylinder, driven by the crankshaft and running in a bath containing an emulsion of water and oil. The eccentrics drive the eccentric cranks, the bright steel rods to the right. The one nearest the camera is for astern running, the other for ahead. Note the oil cups for hand lubrication.

Opposite bottom right. The main engine high-pressure crosshead, 7-inch diameter piston rod and connecting rod with brass top end bearings. Again, all are hand lubricated.

Right upper. A posed photograph showing oiler Ralph Ahlgren about to check by hand the temperature of big end bearings. The idea is to place the hand as shown, near the crank as it rotates towards you, gradually moving the hand between the inside face of the crank and the bearing itself, until the bearing brushes the index finger. You not only feel the temperature, but also get a smear of oil leaking from the bearing: this will appear clear if all is well.

Right lower. The Kingsbury-type main thrust block interposed between the main engine and the propellor shaft. The shafting within the casing has a strong collar with radial white metal bearings either side, as is apparent from the shape of the casting. When the main engine rotates the propellor, it tries to push the ship forward via the shafting. Were it not for the thrust block, this forward thrust would be taken directly by the crankshaft, greatly damaging the engine. The thrust block transmits the propellor thrust directly to the ship's hull. Large bolts secure the thrust block to a very strong steel seating which is integral with the hull. Bearings are fitted to both sides of the collar, as when going astern the propellor tries to pull the shaft and the engine rearwards out of the hull!

Left upper. A view aft down the shaft tunnel. The shafting is 13½ inches in diameter. There is one bearing per length of shafting, with white metal shells on the lower half only, except on the aftermost bearing. The hydraulic pipes to control the steering gear telemotor are secured to the side bulkhead and the steam and exhaust lines to the steering gear are secured overhead. Beneath the black steel floor plates are various pipes including bilge lines and fuel transfer lines. This tunnel runs below numbers 4 and 5 lower holds, and is relatively roomy, the height increasing aft, so that there one can walk upright. It is actually a pleasant place to walk along from the engine room in hot weather, being cool and quiet. At the very end of the shaft is a vertical escape trunk to the aft deckhouse: the only way out of the engine room apart from the regular ladder access from the accommodation, and intended for emergency use. The two coir mats are polishing the rotating shaft.

Left lower. The main centrifugal circulating pump driven by a single-cylinder steam engine, supplying salt water cooling to the main engine condenser (the large yellowish-painted tank in the right background) which has a cooling surface area of 3,000 square feet. In conjunction with the engine-driven air pump, this maintains a vacuum of about 26 inches of mercury at the low-pressure exhaust. Behind the steam engine can be seen the grey-painted hot well/filter tank which receives the condensate prior to it being pumped back to the boilers.

Opposite top left. The two Worthington Simpson main feed pumps mounted back to back against a vertical RSJ pillar. One pump supplies both boilers, drawing from the hotwell and feeding the boilers via a grease trap and an exhaust-steam feed-water heater.

Opposite top right. The boiler forced-draught fan which serves both boiler furnace fronts. This engine is the same size as the one which drives the main circulating pump, thus sharing spare parts. Its speed is controlled by the boiler-room fireman via the small steam valve and extended spindle which can be seen at top left of the picture. It runs almost silently.

Opposite bottom. The three single-cylinder steam-engine-driven d.c. dynamos, each of 20kw at 120 volts, built by the Troy Engine Company, Pennsylvania. Only two are run at any one time, with the third being on standby. This is a very small electrical load for a 10,000 tons deadweight ship but it is adequate as almost all machinery on the vessel is steam powered. The black main switchboard is in the background. Note the shell construction of welded plates with riveted frames.

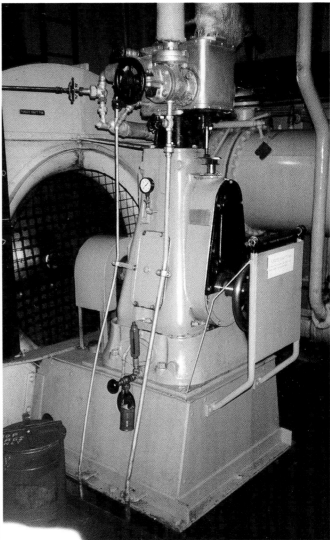

Top. The auxiliary condenser for use in port when the main engine is stopped or when manoeuvring. This condenser receives exhaust from all the auxiliary engines. The double-acting steam engine below drives a condensate pump (right) and a salt-water cooling pump (left).

Middle. Worthington Simpson twin-cylinder bilge and ballast pumps and, to the right, an identical fire pump. The pumps are interchangeable.

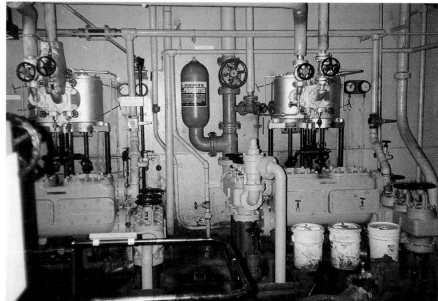

Bottom. The port boiler front. The boiler is a Babcock and Wilcox straight-tube, triple-pass design with superheater. But for the sake of standardisation it was built by Foster Wheeler under licence. Steam pressure is 220 psi, temperature 450F, and steam capacity 24,000 lb/hour. Spare burners can be seen hanging on the central workbench, behind which is the gauge board showing steam pressures and temperatures, feed pressure, forced-draught air pressure and uptake temperature. There is virtually no automation in the operation of the two boilers apart from an oil-fuel heater thermostat.

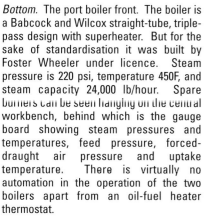

Upper. An overhead view in the boiler room showing the starboard boiler drum and gauge glass (one of two per drum) indicating a half glass of water. The extended spindle controls the auxiliary feed check valve. These are non-return valves mounted on the boiler drum, admitting feed water under high pressure from the feed pump. As their function is so vital, it is customary to provide two. In the previous photograph can be seen both the hand-wheels for the main and auxiliary feed check valves. The valve mounted on the drum is for draining scum from the water surface.

Lower left. The twin-cylinder steam engine by Sumner Iron Works of Washington driving the steering gear. The cranks on this engine are at 90 degrees so there is no 'dead' position from which the engine will not move. The steam valves for rotation in either direction can be controlled by hand from the steering flat or from the emergency steering position above deck or, normally, from the wheelhouse via the hydraulic telemotor system. In the foreground is the geared quadrant connected by shock absorbing springs to the tiller, connected in turn to the rudder post. Should the steering engine be damaged beyond use the quadrant can be moved via a block and tackle and wires connected to the warping winch on deck aft.

Lower right. The original outfit of main engine spanners, still used on engine overhauls.

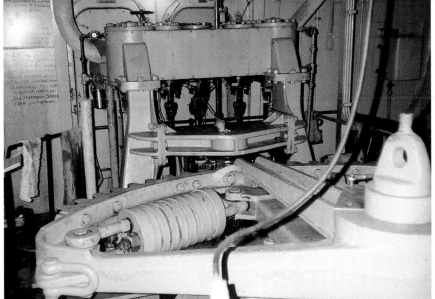

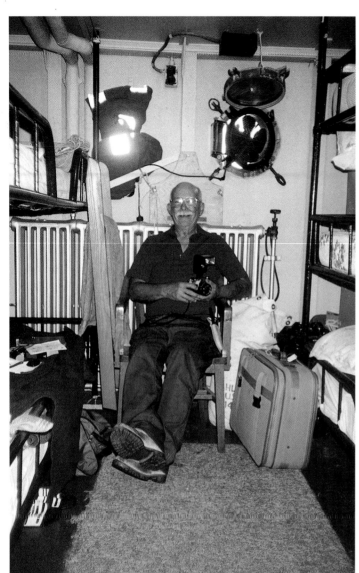

Upper left. The cabin used by the writer, as a fireman/water tender and by oiler Ralph Ahlgren during the 1994 Normandy voyage of *Jeremiah O'Brien*. Like all the ship, this cabin apart from the carpet is in original 1943 condition. With seven bunks, it was used by the defence gunners during the war.

Upper right. The builder's plate mounted on the bridge front. Note the rather substandard, but effective, welding below.

Below. The wheelhouse. Apart from the modern radar in the background this space is in original condition. The telegraph and steering gear controls are extended through the deckhead to the monkey island which is the preferred helm position in good weather. Visibility from here is far superior to that from the wheelhouse which has very small forward facing windows.

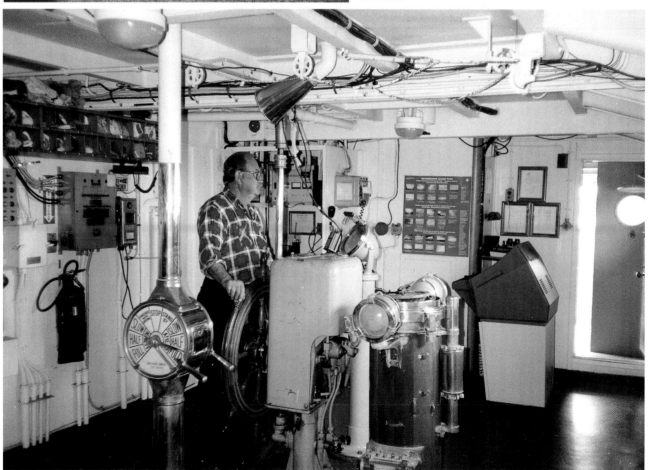

STEAM COLLIER SUNSET

Offered as a finale to our articles on coastal colliers, these splendid photographs show the last two generations of steam ships built for the electricity industry, just as the sun was about to set on this type of ship. Above is *Cliff Quay* (3,357/1950), the first big collier for the newly-constituted British Electricity Authority. Six of this class were built by William Pickersgill and Sons Ltd. at Sunderland, all given triple-expansion engines by the Sunderland shops of North Eastern Marine Engineering (1938) Ltd. Five were withdrawn in 1971 and 1972,

being broken up or in three cases sold for further trading, but *Cliff Quay* steamed on until 1983, when she was broken up at Manchester. She was named after, and frequently served, the power station near Ipswich. *[Roy Fenton collection]*

Sir William Walker (2,901/1954) (below) was the lead ship of five slightly smaller colliers, designed with a narrower beam so they could enter Shoreham. The class had the distinction of being the last ever steam colliers, a breed that could trace its pedigree back to the *John Bowes* of

just over a century earlier. Their appearance benefited from some attention being paid to design details like the funnel shape and treatment of the superstructure. The Austin and Pickersgill-built *Sir William Walker* lasted almost until the end of steam in the coastal coal trade, being sold in 1983 by the then Central Electricity Generating Board just months ahead of the *James Rowan*, last of them all. *Sir William Walker* was towed away to be broken up at Vigo. She is seen at West Leigh Middle Anchorage, off Southend, in June 1982. *[Dave Salisbury]*

OLD WINE, NEW BOTTLES
British cargo liners under old and new colours

In what may end up being an occasional series in *Record,* we compare the appearances of British cargo liners in their vintage post-war years with how they looked after being sold off and repackaged under new colours. Thanks to Dave Salisbury and Paul Boot, who independently suggested this theme and to both these gentlemen and to Jim McFaul and Fred Hawks for supplying colour slides.

ALMEDA STAR and HARLECH
Smith's Dock Co. Ltd., Middlesbrough; 1975, 9,781gt, 156 metres
9-cyl. 2SCSA Burmeister & Wain-type oil engine by J.G. Kincaid and Co. Ltd., Greenock.

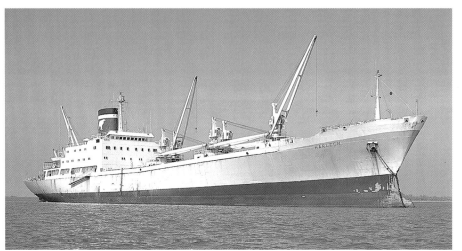

In the 1970s, Blue Star's second 'A' class revived some of the names of their celebrated two funnel passenger ships of the 1920s, all of which were war losses. Five of the six 1970s reefers were built at Middlesbrough, the sixth, oddly, coming from Denmark. Blaming tough market conditions, Blue Star sold off four in 1984 to Hong Kong owners who placed them under the management of Wallems and chartered them back to Blue Star. Several took Scottish-sounding names, *Almeda Star* initially becoming *Arran,* but quickly shifting nominal allegiance to Wales as *Harlech,* as photographed when laid up on the River Blackwater in August 1985. A neat touch was that each of the four carried its own distinctive funnel emblems.

The photos here are out of sequence: *Harlech* later reverted to *Almeda Star* and full Blue Star colours, as seen at Walsoorden on the River Scheldt in July 1998. This reversion raises strong suspicions that the ships never actually left Vestey ownership. *[Both: Dave Salisbury]*

ARCADIAN and BATROUN
Henry Robb Ltd., Leith, 1960, 3402g, 367 feet
7-cyl. 2SCSA Sulzer-type oil engine by the Fairfield Shipbuilding and Engineering Co. Ltd., Govan.

Caught off Erith in the Thames in July 1974, *Arcadian* was the last of the fine, bijou cargo liners built for Ellerman and Papayanni with engines amidships. As the once-enormous Ellerman Group slowly rationalised itself, it was decreed that she should bear a 'City' name, and she became *City of Famagusta,* quite appropriately in view of her Mediterranean trading. Perhaps not surprisingly, Mediterranean owners bought her when Ellerman had done with her in 1977, and T. Gargour et fils of Beirut, Lebanon renamed her *Batroun.* Evidence from this photograph on the Nieuw Waterweg in June 1977 and observations indicate that she was well kept. Unusually, the deep white strake of her Ellerman days has been retained, and she looks as handsome as ever under this ownership, which lasted until 1986 when she was broken up on Gadani Beach. *[Both: Dave Salisbury]*

ASSIOUT and CHRYSSOULA II

Harland and Wolff Ltd., Belfast; 1949, 3,422gt, 367 feet

8-cyl. 4SCSA Burmeister & Wain-type oil engine by Harland and Wolff Ltd., Belfast

In their reorganisation in the early 1970s, the P&O Group seemed determined to extinguish any vestige of individuality in the large number of companies they owned. A tiny spark survived, however. The fleet of the former Moss Hutchison Line Ltd., although formally managed by P&O General Cargo Division from 1971, retained its restrained but distinctive colours, probably until all its ships were sold. Seen here in November 1971, *Assiout* kept her black funnel with white band until sold in August 1973 to the Apolloanav Shipping Co. S.A., managed by Grecomar Shipping Agency Ltd. which hid the identity of one D.N. Leventakis. Her large funnel displays his colourful funnel design well. Photographed deep-laden in the Bosphorus in May 1981, *Chryssoula II* was reaching the end of her career, although her external condition does not suggest this. She was broken up on Gadani Beach later that year. [Assiout: *F.W. Hawks;* Chryssoula II: *Dave Salisbury]*

BENARMIN and YONG CHUN

Charles Connell and Co. Ltd., Glasgow; 1963, 11,362gt, 550 feet

10-cyl. Sulzer-type oil engine by Barclay Curle and Co. Ltd., Glasgow.

One of the great joys of ship watching in the days when British cargo liner fleets were still strong was identifying a ship at a distance, usually from the often-subtle combination of colours each owner employed. The grey hulls and buff funnels of Ben Line might not sound distinctive, but with the company's particular shade of mast colour, and a shallow white strake on the hull, recognition was not difficult. It is interesting to compare the views of *Benarmin* in September 1970 with that of her in Chinese ownership as *Yong Chun* on the Nieuw Waterweg in July 1981. Her hull is still grey (well, mostly grey) and green, but a change of mast colour and deletion of the white strake considerably alters her looks.

Yong Chun's Chinese career was longer than her Ben ownership: sold in 1972 when only nine years old, she lasted in Chinese ownership until 1987. [Benarmin: *George Gould collection, World Ship Photo Library 10601;* Yong Chun: *Dave Salisbury]*

BULIMBA and BUNGA KENANGA
Harland and Wolff Ltd., Govan; 1959, 6,796gt, 427 feet
6-cyl. 2SCSA Burmeister & Wain-type oil engine by Harland and Wolff Ltd., Govan.

Nothing built previously by British India Steam Navigation Co. Ltd. prepared the world for the *Bulimba*. First of a class of five for the Australia-India-Persian Gulf trade, her 'streamlined' design completely broke with BI tradition, and has stood the test of time very well. There were important innovations below the surface, too: accommodation was completely air conditioned, alternating current was employed, and the engine type had never been used by the company before. *Bulimba's* design had the desired effect of drawing attention to her.

The class seems to have given very dependable service - *Bulimba* certainly seems in excellent external condition in this June 1970 view - although all were sold early, after just 12 years' service. *Bulimba* became *Bunga Kenanga* in the fleet of Malaysian International Shipping Corporation, as seen here at Singapore in March 1976. Her new owners gave her a colourful funnel but, robbed of her BI black and generous white, she just never looked as elegant in workaday grey. In 1977 she was sold again to become the *Seasprite,* but as this she became the only member of the class to come to a violent end. On 1st July 1979 she ran aground in the Gulf of Kutch, and was abandoned as a total loss. [Bulimba: *George Gould collection, World Ship Photo Library 15868*; Bunga Keninga: *Dave Salisbury*]

CITY OF CAPETOWN and OTAGOLD
Alexander Stephen and Sons Ltd., Linthouse; 1959, 9914g, 545 feet
12-cyl. 2SCSA Sulzer-type oil engines by Alexander Stephen and Sons Ltd., Linthouse.

When Ellerman Lines began following the trend to superstructure three-quarters aft in the late 1950s, their first essay was the *City of Melbourne,* a ship which reverted to the split-superstructure layout that rather obviated the logic of putting engines so far aft to give clear deck space forward. Built for Ellerman and Bucknall's Australian routes, the big reefer was displaced once refrigerated container ships entered these trades, and was switched to South African services, and appropriately renamed *City of Capetown* as seen here. Her post-Ellerman career was short, just a year as *Otagold* in the ownership of Reefer Lines (Pte.) Ltd., and we are lucky to have such a good shot of her under this name. Indeed, she was probably bound for breakers at Kaohsiung when this photograph was taken of her at Singapore in 1979. She looks a little tired in her pale grey hull, and her masts have probably not seen fresh paint since her Ellerman days. But the elegance of a nicely-designed cargo liner is still apparent, an art which naval architects seem to have lost not long after her completion. [City of Capetown: *Dave Salisbury;* Otagold: *Don Brown*]

CLAN MENZIES and XING LONG

Greenock Dockyard Co. Ltd., 1958, 7,315gt, 503 feet

6-cyl. 2SCSA Doxford-type oil engine by Wallsend Slipway and Engineering Co. Ltd., Wallsend-on-Tyne.

Clan Menzies was the last of Clan Lines' classic cargo liners, with engines truly amidships. With her two sisters, *Clan Malcolm* and *Clan Matheson,* she gave her Glasgow owners 21 years' good service. Seen here off Erith in September 1977, *Clan Menzies* was sold in a deal with *Clan Malcolm,* becoming *Trinity Splendour.* It was originally intended that she would be broken up in the far east, but she was reprieved and operated by China Ocean Shipping Co. as *Xing Long,* as which she was photographed in Hong Kong during November 1980. Where she was eventually broken up is not known, *Lloyd's Register* eventually deleting her for lack of up to date information. She is another case of a fine cargo liner losing some of her attractiveness when dressed in plain grey. *[Both: Dave Salisbury]*

CLAN RANALD and GOLDEN SEA

Greenock Dockyard Co. Ltd., Greenock; 1965, 7,955gt, 529 feet

7-cyl 2SCSA Burmeister & Wain-type oil engine by J.G. Kincaid and Co. Ltd., Greenock.

Four Clan Liners with second names beginning 'R' had the melancholy distinction of being the last class of ships built for Clan, and the last group built at the company's own shipyard, Greenock Dockyard. The 'R' names reflected the Union-Castle tradition of giving its reefers names in 'R', although three had been well used by Clan. Seen here in July 1972, *Clan Ranald* was the fourth of the name. Oddly, Union-Castle did not respect this tradition when the ships were transferred to their ownership, and in 1976 *Clan Ranald* became *Dover Castle,* and in 1979 *Dover Universal.* Sold to London-based Greeks in 1981, she traded as *Golden Sea* for Kappa Maritime Ltd., as seen on the Nieuw Waterweg, freshly painted and looking smart, in July 1981. She was broken up at Gadani Beach in 1985. [Clan Ranald: *George Gould collection, World Ship Photo Library 8735;* Golden Sea: *Dave Salisbury]*

GLENOGLE and YANG CHENG

Fairfield Shipbuilding and Engineering Co. Ltd., Glasgow; 1962, 11,918gt, 544 feet
9-cyl. 2SCSA oil engine by Sulzer Brothers Ltd., Winterthur.

Competition with their old rivals, Ben Line, persuaded Glen Line to build some remarkably fast cargo liners in the early sixties, the four celebrated *Glenlyon* class ships. With a massive 18,000 brake horse power, *Glenogle* achieved 23 knots on trials. Ironically, these Glen Line ships eventually all came under Ben Line control, as the two companies merged their services with the advance of containerisation. *Glenogle* was still in Glen colours when caught off North Woolwich in January 1976.

In 1978 all four were sold, two going to Communist China. *Glenogle* passed through interim ownership by a Hong Kong-based but Chinese-funded company as *Harvest,* before becoming the Shanghai-registered *Yang Cheng,* seen here at the same Thames location in August 1979. Allowing for some rust streaks and the grey hull which lacks the dignity of her Glen colours, she still looks a magnificent, powerful ship, this view emphasising the length of her forward deck.

Yang Cheng was deleted by *Lloyd's Register* in May 2002 because her continued existence was in doubt. Prior to this, lack of definite information about her fate had led to much talk of a preservation attempt. [*Both: Dave Salisbury*]

SCHOLAR and STEEL TRADER

Cammell, Laird Shipbuilding and Engineering Co. Ltd., Birkenhead; 1965, 5,349gt, 457 feet
6-cyl. 2SCSA oil engine by Sulzer Brothers Ltd., Winterthur.

Cunard's last batch of cargo liners had somewhat chequered careers, none lasting long with Cunard, but being transferred to their Brocklebank subsidiary or, in the case of *Samaria,* being sold to Harrison Line after only four years on the London to New York service. Never a company to disdain good secondhand vessels, Harrisons did better with her, and *Scholar* sailed for them for almost ten years, and is seen here on the Thames at Erith in June 1975. In January 1979 she was laid up, but in June was sold to the Brotra Shipping Corporation and renamed *Steel Trader* under the Greek flag. The photograph of her on the Nieuw Waterweg in July 1980 shows few changes in colour, mainly affecting the funnel and masts. It may have been taken on her last voyage, as in August 1980 she was trapped in the Shatt-el-Arab waterway when war broke out between Iran and Iraq. There are suggestions that her burnt-out hulk is still there. [*Both: Dave Salisbury*]

THESSALY and LIHO

Harland and Wolff Ltd., Govan; 1957, 7,299gt, 445 feet

6-cyl. 2SCSA Burmeister & Wain-type oil engine by Harland and Wolff Ltd., Govan

For such a renowned company, the appearance of many of Royal Mail Line's cargo liners was somewhat ordinary, although their Loch vessels featured in *Record 22* were honourable exceptions. Seen here in September 1970, *Thessaly's* appearance did not greatly change after her sale in 1971 apart from altered funnel colours, according to the evidence of this shot of her as *Liho* at Singapore in March 1976. She had an intermediate name, *Japan,* between 1971 and 1976. *Liho* was broken up at Kaohsiung in March 1979.

[Thessaly: *George Gould collection, World Ship Photo Library 15920*; Liho: *Dave Salisbury*]

TURAKINA and PATRICIA U

Bartram and Son Ltd., Sunderland; 1960, 7,707gt, 455 feet

8-cyl. 2SCSA Sulzer-type oil engine by George Clark (Sunderland) Ltd., Sunderland.

The refrigerator ship *Turakina* was a one-off, built as the contribution of the New Zealand Shipping Co. Ltd. to the New Zealand to Japan route of Crusader Shipping Co. Ltd. Compared to contemporary ships being built for her owners, she was one hatch shorter. She is seen in the plain yellow funnel of her owners, which was defaced with a shield whilst on Crusader services. The second photograph shows her at Cuxhaven in June 1979 following her sale to the US-based Uiterwyk Corporation as the Panama-flag *Patricia U.* The white hull does nothing for her appearance, even allowing for the rust-staining, and her distinctly uneven trim tends to exaggerate her top-heavy appearance. She later became *Gulf Reefer* and *Sines,* being broken up in China during 1986.

[Turakina: *World Ship Photo Library 6171*; Patricia U: *Dave Salisbury*]

BIG ICs IN COLOUR

To complement this issue's Fleet in Focus feature are these transparencies of Shaw, Savill's post-war cargo-passenger ships, the 'Big Ics'. Seen above in September 1963, *Athenic,* has already lost one of her pairs of lifeboats, although she continued carrying passengers until 1965. In the lower view her accommodation has been cut back. This is Southampton, 4th March 1969, and she may well be preparing for her last round voyage: she arrived at the breakers' yard in Kaohsiung in October of that year. *[World Ship Society 35056 and Les Ring collection, World Ship Society 6303]*

Ceramic at almost the end of her career - note the uncared for hull - at Liverpool on 13th February 1972 (above). After one further voyage to South Africa she was broken up in Belgium. *[Paul Boot]*

In April 1967, *Gothic* still has two more years service as a cargo vessel ahead of her (below). Note that, unlike *Ceramic*, she still has her full complement of boats, although she ceased carrying passengers in 1965. *[George Gould collection, World Ship Photo Library 11645]*

IRON COLOURS
Flags and funnels of BISCo ore carriers
J.L. Loughran

 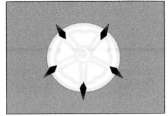

North Yorkshire Shipping Co. Ltd. (Bolton Steam Shipping Co. Ltd., managers), London

 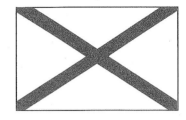

Bowring Steam Ship Co. Ltd. (C.T. Bowring and Co. Ltd., managers), London

Northern Mercantile and Investment Corporation Ltd. (Campbells (Newcastle) Ltd., managers), Newcastle-upon-Tyne

Clyde Shipping Co. Ltd., Glasgow

Hindustan Steam Shipping Co. Ltd. (Common Brothers Ltd., managers), Newcastle-upon-Tyne.

 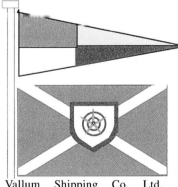

Vallum Shipping Co. Ltd. (Common Brothers Ltd., managers), Newcastle-upon-Tyne

St. Denis Shipping Co. Ltd. (Wm. Cory aand Son Ltd., managers), London

Crest Shipping Co. Ltd., London

Currie Line Ltd., Glasgow

Watergate Steam Ship Co. Ltd. (R. S. Dalgliesh Ltd., managers), Newcastle-Upon-Tyne

 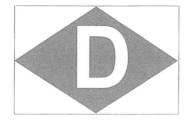

J. and J. Denholm (Management) Ltd.,
Glasgow

H. Clarkson and Co. Ltd., London (J.
and J. Denholm (Management) Ltd.,
Glasgow, managers)

St. Andrews Shipping Co. Ltd. (J. and J.
Denholm (Management) Ltd., managers),
Glasgow

 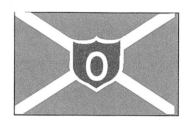

Scottish Ore Carriers Ltd. (J. and J.
Denholm (Management) Ltd.,
managers), Glasgow

 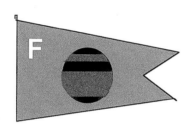

Furness Withy and Co. Ltd., London

Welsh Ore Carriers Ltd. (Gibbs and
Co. (Ship Management) Ltd.,
managers), Newport

Ore Carriers Ltd. (Houlder Bros. and Co.
Ltd., managers), London

 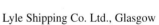

Lyle Shipping Co. Ltd., Glasgow

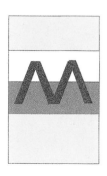 

Falaise Ore Carriers Ltd. (Mavroleon Bros.
(Ship Management) Ltd.), London

Traditional Traders Ltd. (Mavroleon
Bros. (Ship Management) Ltd.,
managers.), London

Naess Denholm and Co. Ltd., Glasgow

St Helens Shipping Co. Ltd., London [Silver Line Ltd]

Bishopsgate Shipping Co. Ltd., London [Silver Line Ltd.]

Bishopsgate Shipping Co. Ltd., London [Silver Line Ltd.]

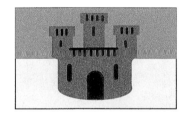

Bamburgh Shipping Co. Ltd. (W.A. Souter and Co. Ltd., managers), Newcastle-upon-Tyne

Sheaf Steam Shipping Co. Ltd. (W.A. Souter and Co. Ltd., managers), Newcastle-upon-Tyne

Louis Dreyfus et Cie., Paris, France

Buries Markes Ltd., London

I/S Farland (Sverre A. Farstad and Co., managers), Aalesund, Norway

A/S Gerrards Rederi, Kristiansand, Norway

 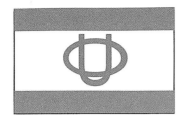

A/S Falkefjell and A/S Dovrefjell (Olsen and Ugelstad, managers), Oslo, Norway

I/S Essex (Bj. Ruud-Pedersen, managers), Oslo, Norway

Victore Jenssens Rederi A/S (Simonsen and Alstrup, managers), Oslo, Norway

A/S Anatina (M. Chr. Stray, managers), Kristiansand, Norway

A/S Ugland's Rederij (J.M. Ugland, managers), Grimstad, Norway

Vesteraalens D/S, Stokmarknes, Norway

In the flesh, as it were, is the funnel of Welsh Ore Carriers Ltd. on *Welsh Herald* at her home port of Newport, Monmouthshire on 5th September 1970. The *Welsh Herald*, below, was photographed again at Newport on 31st July 1969 (see page 211). More ore carriers in full colour over the page. *[World Ship Photo Library 34491 and 34490]*

A fine view of Lyle Shipping's *Cape Howe* on 1¹th July 1969. See page 215 of this issue. *[World Ship Photo Library 34447]*

...is intended to cover Souter's *Bamburgh Castle* in *Record* 25. Here is a preview of her as *Eva* on the ...ieuw Waterweg in July 1980. *[Dave Salisbury]*

...eraklia at Terneuzen on the River Scheldt in April 1988. See page 161 of *Record* 24. *[John Clarkson ...ollection and Dave Salisbury]*

Common Brothers' *Iron Age* is seen left in her original condition, with the slightly rusty hull which ...

Sagamore of Furness Withy and Co. Ltd. photographed on 15th August 1966. See page 211. *[World Ship Photo Library 34487]*

Morar (pages 204 and 210) rebuilt as the motor vessel *Arnis* on the Nieuw Waterweg, 10th June 1970. *[Gould collection, World Ship Photo Library 13793]*

Houlder Brothers managed eight ore carriers of two distinct sizes. Both types are illustrated, the 506-feet *Mabel Warwick* on 3rd July 1970 (left), and the 427 feet *Oregis* on 23rd March 1969 (right). See page 212. *[World Ship Photo Library 34481 and 34478]*

Managed by Denholm for the brokers H. Clarkson and Co. Ltd., London, *Clarkavon* is seen on 9th March 1969. See page 206. *[World Ship Photo Library 34457]*

The sort of shot that makes colour reproduction worthwhile: Denholm's *Wellpark*, 23rd March 1969. See *Record* 23, page 159. *[World Ship Photo Library 34489]*

1968 (left) and *Dunkyle* on 3rd July 1966 (right). *[World Ship Photo Library 34465 and 34471]*

St. Andrews Shipping Co. Ltd. was a joint venture between British Iron and Steel Corporation and Denholms, the latter also managing the ships (see page 207). Seen here are their *Dunadd* on 4th July

Port in Focus
GARSTON
Nigel Bowker

The port of Garston, lying four miles upstream of the Liverpool Docks on the Lancashire side of the Mersey Estuary, was essentially a railway-inspired port. It owes its inception to the competition for the cheapest and most effective means of transporting coal from the extensive fields in the St. Helens area of Lancashire to the Mersey for consumption in Liverpool, by the salt industry on the River Weaver in Cheshire, and for export to Ireland, the Isle of Man and other Irish Sea ports, and in due course as bunkers for steamships.

This country's first canal - the Sankey Brook Navigation - was the pioneer, with its exit locks on to the tidal Mersey gradually moving downstream from Sankey, near Warrington, then Fidlers Ferry and subsequently to Runcorn Gap (Widnes) in 1833 to overcome the poor water levels in the upper river at neap tides, which could effectively prevent any movement of craft.

To combat the monopoly of the Sankey Brook Navigation, the St. Helens and Runcorn Gap Railway was promoted and eventually opened its competing route in 1833 to a new dock at Runcorn Gap on the Mersey, capable of accommodating vessels loading up to 300 tons. At the same time the canal extended its egress point downstream to an adjacent location - just to the westward (see *Record* 10 for photos of the dock and the canal twin exit locks). Both undertakings now shared the same tidal opportunities and problems offered by Runcorn Gap.

As so often happens, after 12 years of rate cutting in order to win a larger share of the traffic on offer, the two enterprises amalgamated to form the St. Helens Canal and Railway Company, after which the combined organization enjoyed a lengthy period of considerable prosperity and a virtual monopoly. Both canal and railway were used and each showed increases in traffic as industry burgeoned in St. Helens and at Widnes, as Runcorn Gap came to be known after 1864. In fact, the railway and canal were the reasons for the development of Widnes - whose name was to become synonymous with the chemical industry and indeed the pungent aromas for which it subsequently become infamous.

However, the vagaries of the ever shifting Upper Mersey channels could still hamper shipping and furthermore imposed a limitation on the size of vessel that could be utilized. Once again attention turned to moving to a further downstream shipping facility, both canal and railway being in turn examined as the means of effecting this extension. Eyes were now firmly focussed on Garston, which up to that point possessed a small tidal dock and a salt works.

By 1853 the railway was extended from Runcorn Gap and Widnes to Garston and the New Dock, on which work had commenced in 1851. This dock - now perversely known as Old Dock - was equipped with high-speed coal drops for loading vessels direct from railway wagons. It was formally opened on 21st June 1853. The dock as built enclosed a water area of six acres and it was reported in the local press of the time that the majority of the stone used in its construction had been excavated from the bed of the River Mersey (one presumes at low water!).

The dock was an immediate success and for the first time since its inception in 1833 the railway carried more tonnage than the canal, although traffic on the latter was still increasing. By 1864 that Victorian commercial giant, the London and North Western Railway Company, had spread its tentacles and identified the St. Helens Canal and Railway Company's Runcorn Gap to Garston line as essential to forming a significant part of a new direct route linking Liverpool to Crewe, London and the south. Initially it leased the line for six months and then made a formal take over.

New investment saw further expansion of the port of Garston as an alternative to its larger neighbour Liverpool which also had significant coal exporting facilities, which were directly accessible by the lines of rival railway companies. In June 1875 the LNWR opened Garston's North Dock which, contrary to its name, was immediately north west of the Old Dock, and was connected to it. Like its older neighbour, it had its own tidal entrance gates and was equipped with coal drops to service the ever-expanding coal trade. This, however, with the LNWR's extensive system, was no longer restricted to the local St. Helens coalfield but could also service Wigan, Manchester, Yorkshire and Midlands pits. Further expansion was planned in 1888 but this did not come to fruition until February 1909 when the Stalbridge Dock (named after Lord Stalbridge, an LNWR director) was opened to the south east of the Old Dock and in the process obliterated the site of the original tidal Salt Dock. Besides being equipped with further coaling facilities - thus giving a total of fourteen railway coal drops between the three docks - Stalbridge was furnished with a proper entrance lock, which eventually led to the closing of the Old and North tidal entrances. It is now fully automated and is the sole access point to the Garston system.

The main trades handled by the port were the export of coal, and the import of timber, bananas and oranges. In later years guntapite from the Irish Republic (roofchrome used for lining furnaces), steel and containers regularly featured in Garston's trade.

A new high-technology rail-fed bulk coal-loading terminal was opened on the north side of Stalbridge Dock on 8th June 1981, replacing the remaining wagon drops on that quay and on the Old Dock. However, with the complete closure of the Lancashire Coalfield and the decimation of the coal mining industry in Britain, this is now mothballed. In an ironic twist of fate that would have been unthinkable thirty years ago, coal is now imported into the Mersey in vast quantities. This is conveyed by bulk carrier from Colombia, the United States, Poland and Russia and is discharged at a purpose-built Mersey Docks and Harbour Company terminal at Liverpool's South Gladstone No 1 Dock at the mouth of the Mersey.

These photographs from the author's collection were taken around Garston Docks in September 1932.

Puriri (8,047/1916) of the Federal Steam Navigation Co. Ltd. is berthed on the south side of Stalbridge Dock, discharging into railway wagons belonging to the LMS and GWR. She is actually wearing the colours of the associated New Zealand Shipping Co. Ltd. to which her nomenclature is more appropriate. Built at Flensburg for Norddeutscher Lloyd as *Augsburg*, she was surrendered to Britain in 1919. She was bought by the Hain Steamship Co. Ltd. in 1920 as *Tremere*, but in 1924 was transferred within the P&O group to Federal and again renamed. *Puriri* was sold for breaking up in Japan during 1934.

On the west side of the dock alongside the banana sheds are three LMS steam dredging hoppers, while a fourth lies astern of the *Puriri* on the south quay. The outermost vessel on the west side is the *Dalmeny* (472/1914) built by C.H. Walker of Sudbrook. Presumably intended for service on the Firth of Forth on account of her name (the southern end of the Forth Railway Bridge in Linlithgow), she was bought by the LNWR and transferred to Liverpool registry in 1921, coincidental with her move south to Merseyside. Transferred to Fleetwood in 1947, she passed into the ownership of the British Transport Commission in 1948, and was broken up at Barrow-in-Furness in 1963. She had a sister vessel built in the same yard named *Queensferry* after the northern landfall of the Forth Railway Bridge in Fife. She too was transferred to Liverpool registry in 1921 and remained under the management of British Transport Docks at Garston until broken up in 1963.

The Old Dock, Garston on 15th September 1932 showing the two southernmost of the four 20-ton balanced coal tips on the east side of the dock. Discharging into railway wagons south of the coal tips is the steamer *Bollsta* (1924/1889), built by Oddens Skipsvaerft at Grimstad, Norway for Fred. Olsen. *Bollsta* was to have an eventful war. On 2nd December 1943 she was in Bari when the brightly-lit Italian port was attacked by over 100 Junkers 88 bombers. In a spectacularly successful raid, the Luftwaffe destroyed at least 20 ships, several of which - including *Bollsta* - were sunk when other ships carrying ammunition exploded. One of these was carrying mustard gas, the release of which added to the horrors of the attack. The hulk of *Bollsta* was raised after the war, and in 1948 it became the *Stefano M* of Genoa, then in 1950 *Sabino*, in 1958 *Coraggioso* of Venice, and was broken up at La Spezia early in 1969.

On the extreme left is one of the London Midland and Scottish Railway Company's steam hopper barges; a fairly elderly one judging by the lack of bulwark plating at the stem. Loading from the southernmost coal drop is an unidentified wooden two-masted topsail schooner, which is using its port anchor as a means of winching itself along the berth to aid loading and trimming of the coals. The forecastle appears to have been substantially built up.

On the west side of the dock an elderly steamer with a substantial timber deck cargo has just commenced discharge, whilst beyond the steel plate railway swing bridge is the Stalbridge Dock. The black-topped yellow funnels of two LMS steam hopper barges can be seen in the Stalbridge entrance lock (one of which is probably the *Dalmeny*) whilst on the banana berth are two Elders and Fyffes steamers, believed to be the *Tetela* (5,389/1926) (outermost, emitting smoke) and *Sulaco* (5,389/1926) innermost on the discharge berth.

The bullnose on the extreme right of the shot is part of the now disused tidal entrance - direct into the Old Dock - made redundant by the construction of the Stalbridge Dock with its own entrance lock which could be used four hours either side of high water.

Greek-owned *Irini* she survived until stranded in fog on the Scheldt in February 1959.

On the south quay the steamer viewed stern on is the *Everonika* (3,743/1906) of Riga. Like many Latvian ships of the period, she was British built, completed as *Don Cesar* for the Buenos Aires and Pacific Railway Co. Ltd. She later became the *Apsley* and then Watts, Watts' *Tottenham* before sale of F. Grauds of Riga in 1930. *Everonika* was seized by the USSR in June 1940, only to be seized in turn by the Germans when in Lubeck exactly a year later. Running as *Irma* she was wrecked near Trondheim in March 1944.

Berthed in the east corner discharging pit props to railway wagons is an elderly steamer, with a distinctive fleur-de-lys on the white funnel band. Berthed outboard are three of the LMS Railway steam hopper barges. The inner most one (whose funnel is just visible to the right of the third 7-ton electric grab crane) being the *H* (591/1927), whilst the one outboard is the *Dalmeny* after just having locked into the system as in the previous shot.

In the 1970s the Dale Street entrance to the docks was still occasionally in use, but it was often said that anyone venturing down there alone at night was a 'brave soul', asking to be ambushed from the heights above!

The railway lines on the viaduct paralleled the quayside lines around the south side of the dock via a sandstone-faced high level embankment, eventually turning south to serve industrial premises around Blackburne Street (which at the turn of the 19th century included the Hamilton Iron Works, the Cornholme Bobbin Works, the Crown Copper Mills, Grayson's shipyard and Garston Tannery).

Stalbridge Dock on 15th September 1932 looking west from above Dale Street. As in the previous illustration, the Elders and Fyffes steamers *Tetela* and *Sulaco* can be seen on the banana unloading berth on the west side, whilst their *Patia* (5,355/1922) is bunkering from the coal drops on the north side of the dock. These three ships were built by Cammell Laird at Birkenhead and formed part of a group of 19 sister ships delivered between 1919 and 1930, said to be the largest group of banana boats ever built. Both the *Sulaco* and the *Patia* were lost during the Second World War, but the *Tetela* survived until 1959 when she was broken up in Belgium.

So busy were the docks at one time that buoys were laid in the middle of Stalbridge Dock as extra accommodation for vessels. In this view F.C. Strick's *Shahristan* (4,552/1911) is moored with bows facing west. Strick ships often brought manganese ore from India to the Mersey from where it was transhipped to the iron works at the small port of Mostyn in North Wales, but equally *Shahristan* could be laid up. Originally *Turkistan*, she was sold to Hamburg Amerika Linie as *Niniva* in 1913, being reacquired by Britain as war reparations and returning to Strick as *Shahristan*. Her subsequent career, mainly under the Finnish flag, was lengthy, and as *Atlanta, Equator, Arator, Tramontana*, and finally the

Much of the same subject material as in the previous illustration but viewed from the west side of Stalbridge Dock looking over to the east corner. This shot shows the four moveable 30-ton coal drops which operated on their own set of quay rails and could serve a number of staithes connected to the extensive railway sidings above, giving a far greater flexibility as well as increased capacity over the fixed facilities to be found in the Old and North Docks.

The three steam hopper barges bear reporting numbers in a similar fashion to the colliers serving the Thames. From left to right *Dalmeny* is '3'; the reporting number of *H* is not visible, whilst the third unidentified hopper carries 'R2'.

The steamer with the fleur-de-lys on the funnel can now be identified as another Latvian, the *Sports* (3,283/1909). Again, she had quite a history: built at Newport News as *Jean*, she ran for the A.H. Bull Steamship Co. Inc. of New York until 1926, when sold to Greek owners who named her *Margarita Calafati* then *Gladstone*. M. Zandberg & Co. of Riga bought her in 1928 and gave her this rather charming name (although it may mean something quite different in Latvian) and painted the red fleur-de-lys on her white funnel band. Her fate was, like *Everonika*, to be seized first by the USSR and then in June 1941 by Germany to become *Magdalena*. But she survived the war, even reverting to *Sports* in 1947 when she briefly came under the control of the Ministry of Transport, in 1952 hoisting the Panama flag under the same name (and, one suspects, ownership by Latvian exiles) before being broken up on the Tyne in 1954. It would be interesting to know how the demands of our former ally the USSR for the return of ships like this were resisted by Britain.

The stem of the *Shahristan* can be seen moored to one of the mooring buoys, whilst on the east quay four 7-ton electric grab cranes comprise some of the port's latest cargo handling equipment.

On 15th September 1932 Elders and Fyffes' *Patia* is bunkering from two of the moveable 30-ton coal drops on the north side of Stalbridge Dock. Noteable features are the watertight hull cargo doors for facilitating the loading of the stems of bananas, the weather deck hinged washport doors - which must have produced some distracting noises when rolling in a beam sea - and necessitated by having solid bulwarks; the splendid bridge wing cabs - equipped with what appears to be 'clear view' screens - and above all the workaday finish of the hull paintwork. Adopting white (actually 'silver grey' - a very light grey which gave the appearance of white to the casual observer) for a coal burning freighter - even if it was a fruit ship - was indeed a courageous choice. The light colour would of course assist in keeping the holds cooler than black in southern climes. This vessel - whilst serving as the fighter aircraft catapult ship HMS *Patia* – was sunk by German air attack off the Northumbrian Coast on 27th April 1941; 39 of the crew losing their lives in the action.

September 1932 (it was after the 15th, as the *Tetela* has sailed) the *Sulaco* is discharging bananas at the sheds on West Stalbridge Dock. The fruit can be seen travelling up the elevator conveyors rigged over number 1 and 2 holds.

Sulaco was lost in mid-Atlantic after being torpedoed by *U 124* whilst sailing in ballast in convoy HX 228 on 20th October 1943 with the loss of 65 lives.

The Stalbridge Dock terminal had opened on 1st January 1912, replacing that previously used at Manchester. Elders and Fyffes ceased using Garston as an importing port in July 1965

Sulaco's cargo is being manually loaded from portable conveyors into wooden-bodied LMS banana vans inside the Stalbridge Dock sheds in readiness for rapid distribution to the home market.

The traditional flat cap is *de rigeur* for the army of labourers. One nevertheless cannot help feeling that it is infinitely preferable in style and respectability to what appears to be its modem day substitute imported from across the pond, but manufactured out east, the IQ-reducing baseball cap. Also notable is the apparent age of the workforce - many would appear to be on the up side of 45 - in what was no doubt a physically demanding job.

The original New Dock, later named Old Dock, also in September 1932, with the high-level railway serving coal drops visible in the distance. To the left is a regular trader to Garston, the Co-operative Wholesale Society's *New Pioneer* (722/1905), readily identifiable because of her Manchester-based owner's practice of painting their ship's initials on their funnels. Sold to Greece in 1939 as *Assimi*, she was sunk by air attack at Krioneri on 23rd April 1941.

Two unidentified steam coasters are probably about to load coal for Ireland once the hopper has completed bunkering: Garston being for many years one of the major west coast ports for coal exports.

THOMAS SKINNER'S CASTLE LINE
Malcolm Cooper

Scotland's Victorian shipowners appear to have suffered from a certain lack of imagination in their choice of ships' names, often adopting naming schemes that were already being employed by others already in business. Turnbull and Martin started building up a fleet of steamers with Scottish shire names in 1877 despite the fact that another Glasgow owner, Thomas Law and Co., was already operating a sizeable Shire fleet of sailing vessels. A year later, Charles Cayzer founded his Clan Line in the same port, although Thomas Dunlop, yet again a Glasgow owner, had started using Clan names for his sailing vessels four years before. Perhaps the widest case of imitation was in the use of Scottish Glen names. McGregor, Gow and Co.'s line of Far Eastern liners was to prove the most durable exponent of this naming scheme, but at the end of the nineteenth century there were four other owners also operating Glen-named fleets. It is thus hardly surprising that Donald Currie, one of the founders of the Union Castle Line, was not alone in naming his vessels after castles. Currie built his first Castle sailing ships in 1863. In exactly the same year, Thomas Skinner of Glasgow also began to build up a Castle Line of sailing vessels. Currie employed castle names from all over Britain, while Skinner used only Scottish ones, but there were overlaps in names. Shipping history, however, is largely the history of success and survival. Currie's creation went on to become a twentieth century household name, while Skinner's did not outlive the Victorian era. Thus, despite the fact that his fleet was roughly the same size as Currie's as late as the mid-1870s, Thomas Skinner and his Castle Line have been all but forgotten today.

The Castle Clippers
Skinner had entered shipowning in the 1850s with the purchase of minority stakes in two wooden sailing vessels, the brig *Alexander Wise* and the ship *Zambia.* In 1861 he made his first move into ship management. In that year, Alexander Stephen built the small iron barque *Dunniker* for a consortium of investors headed by William Main, a master mariner from Kirkcaldy. Skinner, who was one of the consortium, was appointed manager. One further iron barque, *Ann Main,* would come from the same builder for the same group of shareholders in 1868 and Skinner was once again appointed manager. He managed both vessels until superceded by Main himself in 1879. By that time, however, Skinner had built up significant shipowning interests and a distinctive brand name of his own.

Skinner announced his arrival on the shipowning scene on what was, for the age, a fairly dramatic scale. No fewer than four iron sailing ships were built for him at three different Clyde yards in 1863. J.G. Lawrie of Whiteinch launched *Edinburgh Castle* in May. She was followed in the second half of the year by *Roslin Castle* and *Lochleven Castle* from Charles Connell and *Bothwell Castle* from Alexander Stephen. All four vessels were placed in the Far East trade, which was to remain the focus of Skinner's trading activities for the remainder of his life. Although sailing ship construction costs were relatively modest (*Bothwell Castle*, for example, cost £8,845 to build), Skinner did not have the means to finance this building programme on his own. Three of the vessels were actually owned by a partnership formed of Skinner, Archibald Arrol and Walter Birrell of Glasgow and Thomas W. Sweet of London. The fourth was owned on a 64th share basis with multiple small shareholders. Skinner provided management for all four.

Between 1863 and the end of the decade, Skinner ordered another twelve Castle sailing vessels for his fleet, all but two from Glasgow shipbuilders. Although the first four vessels had been iron-hulled, the remainder followed the brief fashion of the decade for composite hulls. *Douglas Castle* arrived from Charles Connell in 1864, followed at the end of the same year by *St. Andrew's Castle* from the Sunderland yard of G.S. Moore. Connell and Moore each provided another vessel in 1865 with *Taymouth Castle* and *Lennox Castle* respectively. Connell added two further vessels in 1866 named *Huntly Castle* and *Wemyss Castle* before building what was to prove his last contribution to the fleet in *Kinfauns Castle* of 1867. Two new names joined the list of Skinner's shipbuilders in 1868, with Barclay Curle building *Loudoun Castle* and Randolph Elder building *Carrick Castle*. Elder provided a further vessel, *Doune Castle,* in 1869 before Skinner returned to one of his earlier builders, Alexander Stephen for the last of his composite clippers, *Norham Castle* and *Brechin Castle.*

The ownership patterns established with the early iron clippers were maintained with the later composite additions, with some vessels being owned by the partnership and some by a larger group of 64th shareholders. John Black of Glasgow replaced Thomas Sweet in the partnership-owned vessels in 1866. Skinner's personal stakes in the other vessels varied considerably. For example, he owned only four shares in *Lochleven Castle,* but a varying stake of between 22 and 26 in *St. Andrew's Castle.* The ships themselves were deployed in trades to the east, including China, the East Indies and the Antipodes. As such they were occasional participants in the China tea trade, although Skinner's clippers were not of the 'extreme' variety and thus did not feature in the lists of quick passages or the races to bring the first tea crops of the year home. Interestingly enough in the light of future developments, Skinner maintained a good safety record in these early days, losing only one vessel before 1870, *Taymouth Castle,* which was wrecked off Ireland in 1867 while outward bound for Singapore.

The move to steam
Skinner was one of a number of shipowners to see the potential for introducing steam to the Far East trade following the opening of the Suez Canal and the development of the compound steam engine. His last composite sailing ship order, *Brechin Castle,* was sold while still on the stocks, possibly to free up capital for a move into steam. Skinner's early correspondence with the firm that was to become his major steamship builder indicates that he was originally intending to enter the Australian trade, but he soon shifted attention to the China market where the tea business offered prospects of good economic returns. The Glasgow pioneers in this trade were James McGregor and Leonard Gow, partners in the small firm of A.C. Gow and Co., who built their first iron steamship *Glengyle* in 1870 and put her on the China route after an inaugural voyage to India. Skinner followed suit soon thereafter, ordering a pair of steamers from the yard of J. and G. Thomson, which at that stage was still located on the south bank of the Clyde at Govan, near the London and Glasgow Company yard where McGregor and Gow were building their ships. The first vessel, *Gordon Castle,* was launched on 7th August 1871 and completed in November of the same year. She was followed down the slips by *Drummond Castle* on 28th December, the latter vessel being delivered in March 1872.

The centre of the China trade was London, the largest market for the China teas which provided the most important source of cargoes and revenues, and soon after the delivery of his first two steamers Skinner opened a London office, moving south himself to run it. He would be followed within two years by James McGregor, but initially Skinner acted as London agent for the firm that was to become his deadliest rival, advertising outward Glen sailings as part of his Castle Line service until the end of 1873. By this time J. and G. Thomson had delivered a second larger pair of vessels, *Braemar Castle* and *Cawdor Castle* for Skinner's fleet, the lead vessel actually being the first to be completed at the shipyard's new site at Clydebank. Thomson's relocation to Clydebank delayed the delivery of the two ships, work on which was actually begun at the old Govan yard and then transferred to the new site. *Braemar Castle* was first laid down in April 1872 but not delivered until May 1873, while *Cawdor Castle,* which had actually been laid down first in February 1872 was not delivered until July 1873.

Skinner, like McGregor, but very much in contrast to their Liverpool-based opponent Alfred Holt and Co., appears from the outset to have seen speed as the most important competitive weapon in the China trade. This was not perhaps surprising given the primacy of the homeward trade in tea and the premium revenues to be earned by the winner of the annual race to get the first teas of the season onto the London market. Skinner, however, seems to have taken the need for speed to greater extremes than any of his rivals, and it is tempting to think that this was a product of his experience as a clipper ship owner. A Castle Line advertisement of 1st January 1873 for an outward sailing of *Gordon Castle* was typical of the approach taken: 'This well-known steamer is confidently recommended to intending shippers and passengers, her last passage having been made in 44 days from Hong Kong, including all stoppages.'

Troubles ahead

Skinner's appetite for speed was soon to get him in trouble, or to be more accurate, to be the source of his misfortunes in the eyes of his competitors. On 31st May 1873, at the start of only her second season, *Drummond Castle* was wrecked in Chinese coastal waters homeward bound from Hankow with a cargo of tea. All were saved, and accidents such as this were by no means uncommon in waters that were as yet poorly charted. John Swire, Holt's agent in China and the eventual founder of the Far East freight conference, did, however tell Holt that he was far from surprised by the disaster, ascribing it directly to Skinner's dangerous pursuit of fast passages.

By this time, Thomsons' correspondence with Skinner shows that his relationship with his shipbuilder, upon whom he had depended to raise a significant part of the capital required to build the fleet, was already under serious strain. In October 1872, for example, Thomsons took exception to allegations that he had been 'exceedingly ill used' by them, and claims that 'the worry and torment we have occasioned you will soon terminate your existence'. Clearly exasperated, they replied:

'We have built you a couple of good boats, which everyone who knows a good boat pronounces unequalled in the trade. We have got up your Company, undertaking a serious responsibility in doing so (which the fact of assistance from kind friends does not divest of its importance) and all this with the result we are sorry to say of heavy pecuniary loss to ourselves, and yet you seem to think it becoming to allude to us as ignoramuses in our trade and our whole conduct from beginning to end of a nature "perfectly unbearable".'

In the short term there was no sign of Skinner being badly set back by loss or dispute with his builders and backers. Fleet expansion continued, with two more new steamers joining the fleet in 1874, *Glamis Castle* from Aitken and Mansel and *Fleurs Castle* once again from J. and G. Thomson. Only three years had separated the launching of the first and the sixth steamers, but more than another two were to elapse before a seventh would follow. There were several reasons for this. The shipping world in general was hit by a sharp depression in 1875, and with revenues falling many owners had to rein in their expansion plans. As an example, *Gleneagles,* the Glen Line's eighth new steamer was being advertised in 1874 but was not actually delivered until 1877. At one stage in 1875, Skinner was briefly in abortive negotiations through Thomsons to take over Cunard's *Saragossa* to meet his tonnage needs. Later in the same year he was even requesting quotations for ironclads and gunboats for an unspecified foreign power!

Skinner had also been seeking a simultaneous expansion of his sailing fleet, and through that an entry into the Australia and New Zealand emigrant trade. Three large new iron sailing vessels were completed for him in 1875, two by Thomas Wingate (*Culzean Castle* and *Brodick Castle*) and one by J. and G. Thomson (*Dunnottar Castle*), and more were planned. In a deteriorating trade environment it soon became clear that he had over-committed himself. Thomsons complained that they had been forced to take a larger stake (15/64ths) in *Dunnottar Castle* than they wished to hold and the further orders had to be cancelled. In addition, the bad luck that was already beginning to dog the steam fleet hit the new sailing ships from the start. One of the Wingate vessels, *Culzean Castle,* disappeared without trace on the outward leg of her maiden voyage. The other, *Brodick Castle,* was dismasted and had her master seriously injured soon after leaving the Channel, and was only saved through the heroism of her mate. The 1870s also saw further losses from the older part of the sailing fleet, most of which was now also largely deployed in the

Gordon Castle after sale to McLean and Co., whose houseflag she is flying from her mainmast. *[World Ship Photo Library, courtesy A.J. Smythe]*

Antipodes trade. *Loudoun Castle* was abandoned off Formosa in 1871, *Bothwell Castle* sold, possibly after damage, in 1872 and *Lochleven Castle* was abandoned off Chile in 1879.

Just before Skinner's seventh new steamer, another *Loudoun Castle,* finally arrived at the beginning of 1877, he had suffered a second loss from his steam fleet. *Cawdor Castle* was wrecked in the Hooghly on 7th October 1876 while proceeding downriver from Calcutta on a voyage to Colombo. As she was actually in charge of a river pilot, it is difficult to ascribe her loss to dangerous practice on the part of the company, but the fact that she was engaged on an intermediate voyage separate from the mainstream liner service was indicative of another problem. Skinner's vessels never really succeeded in working their way into the heart of the Far East to UK liner trade. It was significant that when the Far East freight conference was formed in the late 1870s, the Castles participation in it was on the basis of lower homeward conference freights than were allowed to Holt's Blue Funnel or the Glen Line. When the conference experienced one of its periodic disruptions in 1880, its founder Swire identified the Castles as the ships most likely to suffer in a rate war. Skinner also appears to have been experiencing difficulties on the outward route. Unable to find sufficient cargo in competition with P&O, Glen and Jenkins' Shire Line, the Castle steamers started making outward calls at Cardiff to take cargoes of coal. Rates for such freight were significantly lower than for normal outwards cargo, and it is doubtful if Skinner's ships will always have been able to cover their costs.

Against this background, *Loudoun Castle* can be seen as an attempt to restore the firm's flagging fortunes by building a record-breaker. Coming once again from J. and G. Thomson, she was equipped with a 400 NHP compound engine, fully a third greater in power than that of her immediate predecessor. She also sported a clipper bow and figurehead in contrast to the more workmanlike straight stem of her predecessors. In the speed contest she was an immediate, if short-lived success. She won the 1877 tea race with a homeward passage of 41 days, taking five days off the record of the Glen Line's *Glenartney* that had held the title for the previous three years. This, however, was to be Skinner's only success of the decade. *Gleneagles* took back the lead for Glen in 1878 and in the following two years a newer and even faster Glen vessel *Glencoe* took the honours. To add injury to insult, *Loudoun Castle's* 1879 tea sailing was ruined by a serious grounding in the river near Wuhu, while *Glamis Castle* was severely damaged outward bound in a collision with Royal Mail's *Mondego* off Portugal.

The arrival of *Glencoe* brought the McGregor, Gow fleet to 11. With the arrival of *Loudoun Castle* having been balanced by the loss of *Cawdor Castle,* Skinner's steam fleet was only five-strong. The sole immediate reinforcement came from his first and only move into the second-hand market. The steamer *Burmese* had been completed in 1874 for a North Shields owner, but had spent much of her life on charter to companies operating on the UK to Far East route. Skinner had been among her charterers, and purchased her outright in 1879. Renamed *Kenmure Castle,* she was re-registered at London, thus becoming the first ship in the Castle fleet not to appear on the Glasgow registry. She was also the smallest (and probably the slowest) steamer in the fleet, and while she was perfectly suited to the demands of the trade she was unlikely to play a major part in restoring the firm's fortunes.

Unfortunately the fleet was soon to be reduced to five again. On the night of 29th October 1880 *Braemar Castle* was run down by the Shire Line steamer *Breconshire* while lying at anchor in Penang harbour. An attempt was made to tow the stricken vessel ashore, but she foundered in deep water before safety could be reached. Initially it was hoped that she could be raised, but these plans were abandoned as she sank into the muddy bottom athwart the tide. Some of her homewards bound cargo was salved, but at the end of the year the local salvage association had to confess to the owner that it could not find a ship to carry that which could not be sold locally because it emitted 'a horrible stench'.

The last hurrah

Skinner made one last attempt to revive his fortunes in 1881-2, adding three new ships to his fleet. Two were a mis-matched pair from the Middlesbrough shipyard of Raylton Dixon. *Bothwell Castle,* the first to be delivered in April 1881, was an elegant clipper-bowed vessel boasting a full figurehead of Mary Queen of Scots. *Minard Castle,* completed eleven months later was a more powerful vessel of roughly the same hull dimensions, but without the archaic design features. Each ship cost £44,800 to build. The third vessel, delivered between the Middlesbrough pair, was far more expensive to build. She was to prove Skinner's most famous ship, but she was also to be his most expensive mistake.

Despite the superficial design peculiarities of the former, *Bothwell Castle* and *Minard Castle,* were fairly conservative investments. They were actually significantly smaller, less powerful and less expensive than the 1881 new arrivals at the Glen Line, *Glenfruin* and *Glenavon.* Glen, however, was building an even larger and faster vessel, to be called *Glenogle,* in an attempt to maintain its series of record breakers. Skinner's other new building marked a deliberate attempt to beat Glen at its own game and introduce a ship that was far faster than any conventional cargo liner. *Stirling Castle* was launched by John Elder's Govan yard on 21st January 1882 and sailed from the Clyde for China on 23rd March. At over 400 feet long and over 4,000 tons gross measurement, this two-funnelled vessel was easily the largest Skinner ever owned. What really set her apart was her huge compound steam engine, rated at an incredible 1,500 nominal horsepower and capable of driving her at speeds of 17-18 knots. Such size and speed did not come cheap. At £140,800 she cost in excess of 50% more than the two other new vessels together.

The short career of *Stirling Castle* in Skinner's colours is relatively well known. She comfortably outpaced *Glenogle* and all other rivals in the 1882 tea race, reducing the record for a homeward passage to 30 days, seven days better than *Glencoe's* previous year's performance and four days better than even *Glenogle* could manage. In 1883, with extra shifts of stokers aboard, she did even better, taking another day off the record. It was all, however, an exercise in financial futility. Those huge engines were really a step beyond the commercial viability of compound steam technology, and the ship could not hope to earn enough to cover her huge fuel bills let alone amortize her inflated capital cost. Skinner had transferred his three new buildings to separate single ship limited companies soon after their arrival. This may have been an attempt to increase the vendibility of the shares themselves. A single 64th share in *Stirling Castle* was worth £2,200, well beyond the means of the normal shipping investor. It may also have reflected a desire to protect his own increasingly stretched financial position. *Stirling Castle* was registered with £41,800 worth of shares in the name of William Pearce, managing director of Elder's shipyard. It is doubtful whether Pearce saw these as a permanent investment. They probably represented something more like short-term capital to finance construction, and Pearce almost certainly expected his money back reasonably quickly. Skinner did buy back just under a third of Pearce's holding in May 1883, in the process increasing his personal stake in *Stirling Castle* alone to £83,300. He would not appear to have been able to maintain this position, and by the end of the year he had been forced to sell his new flagship.

Disaster and decline

Before *Stirling Castle* left the fleet, however, Skinner's business had been hit by a series of disasters that would probably have ruined his business even if his largest vessel had not proved such a white elephant. Between July 1882 and April 1883 no fewer than three of the seven other steamships of the Castle Line were lost. The first to go was *Fleurs Castle,* wrecked in a storm near Cape Guardafui with the loss of 27 lives on 9th July 1882. Her 18 survivors were looked after by local Arabs and were only picked up by Holt's *Antenor* several weeks after her loss. Worse was to come, as *Kenmure Castle* was overwhelmed by a gale in the Bay of Biscay on 2nd

February 1883. The ship was in trouble from 6 pm on the evening of the 1st when, having already been buffeted by a south west gale for some hours, she was struck from astern by a huge wave which broached her deckhouse. Water began to flood into the after part of the hull. About midnight the screw of the wheel-chain parted, and at 3 o'clock on the morning of 2nd February the deck-house moved bodily. With flooding continuing, the port cutter with 18 aboard was got away, but the ship foundered before another could be launched, taking the master and the rest of the crew with her. The boat was finally picked up by a French steamer on the morning of the 4th, but by this time the second officer had gone mad and jumped overboard. The last disaster occurred on the morning of 10th April 1883 when the one-year old *Minard Castle* sank in deep water after striking a submerged rock near the Island of Cheung Chau in the West Lamma Channel off the Chinese coast. On this occasion, there were no casualties, although the master was deemed to have been at fault for leaving the ship in charge of the third officer in tidal pilotage waters and had his certificate suspended for nine months.

There was really no way back from this triple tragedy. *Stirling Castle* was sold in October 1883 to M. Bruzzo and Co., of Genoa, reducing the steam fleet to only four vessels. There were no further replacements, and Skinner had effectively been reduced to a marginal participant in the Far East trade. Skinner himself died on 2nd August 1884 at his South Kensington home, leaving the business to his three sons, George William, William Auchinloss and Thomas the Younger. He also left a not inconsiderable estate of £72,182 11s 5d, although most of this must have been tied up in shares in the surviving ships. In 1887 his sons disposed of most of the remnants of the fleet. *Loudoun Castle* was sold to another Italian owner, while the two oldest steamers *Gordon Castle* and *Glamis Castle* went to Scottish owners. The remaining sailing ships (whose number had been further reduced by the loss of *St. Andrew's Castle* in 1881 and *Dunnottar Castle* in 1886) were gradually disposed of over the same period. Thomas Skinner and Co. were left only as managers of *Bothwell Castle*, and of the small Anglo-Scandinavian Shipping Company, managed for a third party.

Bothwell Castle's final exit from the fleet was a prolonged process. In 1889 her owners had been forced to face up to reality, reducing the capital of her owning company from £44,800 to £16,000, and the 640 shares from £70 to £25. Only £6 per share was returned to holders at the time, leaving them with a £39 per share (or £24,960 total) capital loss. The ship had ended its last normal China passage at London on 1st August 1886. Thereafter her employment pattern more resembled that of a tramp than a cargo liner, comprising a mixture of UK-Australian passages, trading in the China Sea and the Indian Ocean, and a time charter to the Union S.S. Co. of New Zealand. In April 1892, McIlwraith and McEacharn

bought an 18/64ths interest in the ship and effectively became her co-managers. *Bothwell Castle* spent some time laid-up or under repair in Australia. Her new joint owners found her to be in a 'very bad state', with her condenser looking as though it had not been examined when the ship was new, and the shaft out of line and needing to be lifted out and relined. In February 1895 a Melbourne firm of solicitors were authorised to sell Skinner's remaining interest in the ship for not less than £9,000. This interest was finally bought in January 1896 by McIlwraith and McEacharn who were keen to exercise complete control over a vessel that had already made several passages on their service to Western Australia. This transaction finally brought the shipowning actives of Thomas Skinner and Co. to an end.

Four of the five Castle steamships still afloat when Skinner died enjoyed long second careers. The only early casualty was *Glamis Castle*. She was bought by Donaldson Brothers, renamed *Circe* and placed on their Canadian service, but was wrecked on Anticosti Island in the Gulf of St. Lawrence on 18th July 1891. *Gordon Castle*, the other vessel to return to Scottish ownership, lasted until 1900. She served without change of name in the small Glasgow tramp fleet of Niel McLean until being sold by court order at Cape Town in 1897. She then joined the rapidly growing Glasgow fleet of Maclay and McIntyre, but was sunk with all hands in a collision in Cardigan Bay on 10th September 1900. The other three vessels lasted well into the twentieth century. *Stirling Castle*, fittingly, had the most colourful career. Her Italian owners renamed her *Nord America*, but were sufficiently taken with the reputation earned by the ship under her original name that they displayed both names on the bows. She actually made a brief return to the Red Ensign in 1885 when Adamson and Ronaldson of London acquired her to undertake Admiralty charters as a troopship during the Egyptian crisis of that year. She was briefly re-registered at Malta, but at the end of the year was sold back to her previous Italian owners. She spent most of her new career carrying passengers to South America, but also made some appearances on the North Atlantic route. Back on the southerly route and reduced to a cargo-only role, she stranded near Cape Spartel on 2nd December 1910 and was only refloated to be taken back home for demolition. *Loudoun Castle*, Skinner's previous attempt to build a record-breaker, also served under Italian colours in the South Atlantic. Renamed *Marco Minghetti* by Nav. Gen. Italiana, she kept this name with two subsequent Italian owners and was finally broken up in 1923. The year before the other survivor had also gone to the breakers. *Bothwell Castle* was renamed *Coolgardie*

253

in 1899, and lasted with McIlwraith and McEacharn until 1913, ironically serving as a running mate for part of the time with an old rival, Glen Line's former *Glenfruin,* now renamed *Kalgoorlie.* After McIlwraith and McEachern sold her, she had a succession of other Australian owners before she was sold for debt at Marseilles in 1922 and broken up in Italy.

It is difficult through the mists of time to come to a fair judgement on Thomas Skinner. His surviving correspondence with J. and G. Thomson casts him as an aggressive and sometimes erratic client, always arguing over specifications and costs, and always quick to blame his misfortunes on others.

Contemporary judgements that he was pursuing dangerously aggressive business policies might well have had an element of truth in them. His largest investment was certainly an expensive failure that took the technology of compound steam propulsion beyond the economic limits of the trade he was in. His steam fleet also had an appalling safety record, with six of its eleven vessels being lost within a period of just under ten years. Of his six losses, however, only the first and the last might on the face of things be ascribed to reckless navigation. Whatever his other failings, Skinner does appear to have been very unlucky.

Bothwell Castle soon after her sale to Australia and renaming *Coolgardie.* Later photographs (see page 258) show her without the yards on the foremast. *[Ian Farquhar collection]*

FLEET LIST

1. EDINBURGH CASTLE 1863-1885 Iron ship/barque.
O.N. 45971 627t 175.5 x 29.3 x 18.7 feet.
5.1863: Launched by J.G. Lawrie, Whiteinch.
11.6.1863: Registered at Glasgow in the names of Thomas Skinner, Archibald Arrol, William Birrell and Thomas Whittle Sweet.
8.1875: Converted to barque rig.
16.11.1885: Sold to Gifford Nicholson (subsequently Nicholson and McGill), Liverpool.
19.11.1885: Register transferred to Liverpool.
15.1.1888: Stranded at entrance to Warrnambool harbour, Victoria.
21.1.1888: Abandoned as a total wreck.
24.2.1888: Register closed.

2. ROSLIN CASTLE 1863-1885 Iron ship/barque.
O.N. 45990 644t 183.0 x 31.0 x 17.9 feet.
8.1863: Launched by Charles Connell and Co., Overnewton (Yard No. 11).
14.9.1863: Registered at Glasgow in the names of Thomas Skinner, Archibald Arrol, William Birrell and Thomas Whittle Sweet.
2.1874: Converted to barque rig.
16.11.1885: Sold to Gifford Nicholson (subsequently Nicholson and McGill), Liverpool (register remained at Glasgow).
1889: Sold to J.H. Tandonnet Freres, Bordeaux, France and renamed TAHITI.

20.3.1889: Register closed.
1892: Sold to F. Schultze, Rostock, Germany.
1895: Sold to Ernst Burchard and Co., Rostock.
1897: Sold to H. Janetsky, Rostock.
1899: Sold to Union Chargeurs Coloniaux, Nantes, France and renamed LE MARIN.
6.1909: Broken up.

3. BOTHWELL CASTLE (1) 1863-1872 Iron ship.
O.N. 47822 592t 170.0 x 28.0 x 18.4 feet.
14.10.1863: Launched by A. Stephen and Sons, Kelvinhaugh (Yard No. 43).
4.11.1863: Registered at Glasgow in the names of Thomas Skinner, Archibald Arrol, William Birrell and Thomas Whittle Sweet.
2.1.1872: Sold to Ebenezer Watt and Alexander Denny, Glasgow.
19.12.1873: Sold to Waddle and Russell, Newcastle New South Wales (agents appointed to sell vessel at Sydney, New South Wales for not less than £8,800 on 12.8 and 3.10.1873).
31.12.1873: Re-registered at Newcastle, New South Wales.
1876: Sold to J. and A. Brown, Newcastle, New South Wales and converted to barque rig at Yokohama.
21.12.1884: Wrecked on Ngareik Island, Caroline Group.
30.4.1885: Register closed.

Edinburgh Castle towards the end of her career, after reduction to a barque. *[State Library of Victoria copy H99.220/394]*

4. LOCHLEVEN CASTLE 1863-1879 Iron ship.
O.N. 47825 602t 180.2 x 28.1 x 18.2 feet.
14.11.1863: Launched by Charles Connell and Co., Overnewton (Yard No. 12).
28.12.1863: Registered at Glasgow in the name of Thomas Skinner.
4.1877: Converted to barque rig.
24.8.1879: Abandoned off south coast of Chile.
3.12.1879: Register closed.

5. DOUGLAS CASTLE 1864-1884 Composite ship/barque.
O.N. 50359 678t 176.6 x 30.6 x 18.7 feet.
15.10.1864: Launched by Charles Connell and Co., Overnewton (Yard No. 28).
14.11.1864: Registered at Glasgow in names of Thomas Skinner, William Birrell and Archibald Arrol.
7.1876: Converted to barque rig.
28.3.1884: Sold to James Casey, London.
19.4.1884: Transferred to London register.
1884: Sold to the West of England Shipping Co. Ltd., Plymouth.
12.1887: Sold to G. Brandi and Co., Thisted, Denmark.
6.12.1887: Register closed.
23.6.1891: Last heard of bound to Valparaiso from Swansea with coal.

6. ST. ANDREW'S CASTLE 1865-1883 Composite ship.
O.N. 50374 639t 168.8 x 30.3 x 18.2 feet.
11.1864: Launched by G.S. Moore and Co., Sunderland.
18.1.1865: Registered at Glasgow in name of Thomas Skinner.
15.11.1883: Foundered after collision with the barque GALATEA (which also foundered) of Dundee in Bay of Biscay in position 47 north by 9 west whilst on a voyage from Middlesbrough to the River Plate.
4.2.1884: Register closed.

7. TAYMOUTH CASTLE 1865-1867 Composite ship.
O.N. 52623 627t 172.0 x 29.0 x 18.0 feet.
8.7.1865: Launched by Charles Connell and Co., Overnewton (Yard No. 34).
1.9.1865: Registered at Glasgow in names of Thomas Skinner, Archibald Arrol and William Birrell.
5.1.1867: Wrecked between Tor Point and Tornamoney, County Antrim whilst on a voyage from Glasgow to Singapore with a cargo of casks and bale goods.
25.2.1867: Register closed.

8. LENNOX CASTLE 1865-1885 Composite ship/barque.
O.N. 52624 693t 178.6 x 30.1 x 18.9 feet.
8.1865: Launched by G.S. Moore and Co., Sunderland.
8.9.1865: Registered at Glasgow in name of Thomas Skinner.
11.1875: Converted to barque rig.
21.5.1886: Sold to Henry George Brown, London.
26.5.1886: Sold to Thomas Goldfinch, Whitstable.
9.1886: Broken up.
3.9.1886: Register closed.

9. HUNTLY CASTLE 1866-1884 Composite ship/barque.
O.N. 53382 623t 169.0 x 29.0 x 18.2 feet.
2.1.1866: Launched by Charles Connell and Co., Overnewton (Yard No. 37).
2.2.1866: Registered at Glasgow in the name of Thomas Skinner.
5.1876: Converted to barque rig.
3.1883: Sold to James Casey, London.
6.3.1883: Transferred to London register.
4.1883: Sold to Joseph Hossack, Liverpool.
26.4.1883: Transferred to Liverpool register.
6.4.1887: Condemned and abandoned as a wreck at Calcutta, register closed.
2.5.1887: Repaired and restored to register at Calcutta under ownership of Hajee Mahomed Essack and Co., Calcutta.
1893: Sold to Multick Toajar Naserbin and Mahomed bin Ibrahim bin Abbas, Linga and renamed ATIET ROHOMAN.
13.10.1893: Register closed.
1899: Out of Lloyd's Register.

10. WEMYSS CASTLE 1866-1887 Composite ship/barque.
O.N. 56157 715t 183.0 x 31.0 x 17.9 feet.
24.10.1866: Launched by Charles Connell and Co., Overnewton (Yard No. 40).
19.11.1866: Registered at Glasgow in the name of Thomas Skinner.
4.1883: Converted to barque rig.
25.3.1887: Sold by public auction at St. Thomas.
5.5.1887: Register closed.
1890: Broken up.

11. KINFAUNS CASTLE 1867-1884 Composite ship/barque.
O.N. 58354 799t 187.6 x 32.4 x 19.4 feet.
1.10.1867: Launched by Charles Connell and Co., Overnewton (Yard No. 50).
13.11.1867: Registered at Glasgow in name of Thomas Skinner.
9.1876: Converted to barque rig.
29.8.1884: Condemned and sold at public auction at St. Catharina to C. Abranches and Co., Lisbon, Portugal and renamed MARIANINHA.
15.10.1884: Register closed.
1890: Out of Lloyd's Register.

12. LOUDOUN CASTLE (1) 1868-1871 Composite ship.
O.N. 60379 926g 895n 197.8 x 34.0 x 19.5 feet.
21.8.1868: Launched by Barclay, Curle and Co., Stobcross (Yard No. 175).
29.9.1868: Registered at Glasgow in name of Thomas Skinner.
27.7.1871: Abandoned at sea near South Cape, South Formosa.
20.11.1871: Register closed.

13. CARRICK CASTLE 1868-1885 Composite ship.
O.N. 60387 904g 879n 197.5 x 34.0 x 19.6 feet.
10.1868: Launched by Randolph, Elder and Co., Govan (Yard No. 93).
30.10.1868: Registered at Glasgow in name of Thomas Skinner.
11.1885: Sold to Spanish government and commissioned as the naval training ship NAUTILUS.
5.12.1885: Register closed.
1925: Out of service.
1932: Sold for scrap.

14. DOUNE CASTLE 1869-1887 Composite ship/barque.
O.N. 60415 911g 886n 197.1 x 34.0 x 19.8 feet.
18.3.1869: Launched by Randolph, Elder and Co., Govan (Yard No. 94).
15.4.1869: Registered at Glasgow in name of Thomas Skinner.
1875: Converted to barque rig.
15.12.1886: Sold to J.B. Foley and Co., London.
17.12.1888: Transferred to London register.
1894: Sold to J.A. Ferreira and Co., Lisbon and renamed FLORINDA.
29.1.1894: Register closed.
14.12.1904: Caught fire and sank 16 miles west of St. Paul de Loanda whilst on a voyage from Lisbon with a cargo of coke and kerosene.

15. NORHAM CASTLE 1869-1887 Composite ship/barque.
O.N. 60427 735g 698n 177.4 x 32.1 x 18.0 feet.
4.1869: Launched by A. Stephen and Sons, Kelvinhaugh (Yard No. 128).
25.6.1869: Registered at Glasgow in name of Thomas Skinner.
1873: Converted to barque rig.
21.4.1886: Sold to Peter Holme, Seacombe, Cheshire (register remained at Glasgow).
17.6.1886: Sold to the Norham Castle Ship Co. Ltd. (Philip Hebden Cowley, manager), Liverpool.
15.6.1887: Management transferred to Peter Holme, Liverpool.
10.1887: Wrecked near Punta Lara, River Plate whilst on a voyage from Buenos Aires to Calcutta in ballast.
9.1.1888: Register closed.

16. BRECHIN CASTLE Composite ship.
O.N. 63735 1,057g 1,000n 203.2 x 35.2 x 20.1 feet.
23.11.1869: Launched by A. Stephen and Sons, Kelvinhaugh (Yard No. 129) having been laid down for Thomas Skinner but sold on the stocks to Gregor Turnbull.
25.1.1870: Registered at Glasgow in names of Gregor Turnbull and James Greig.
6.8.1880: Lost off the Cape of Good Hope.
28.10.1880: Register closed.

The Spanish naval training ship *Nautilus*, previously the *Carrick Castle*. [State Library of Victoria copy H99.220/3753]

17. GORDON CASTLE 1871-1887 Iron steamer.

O.N. 63855 2,045g 1,295n 307.7 x 34.3 x 25.4 feet.
C. 2-cyl. by J. and G. Thomson and Co., Glasgow; 255 NHP.
7.8.1871: Launched by J. and G. Thomson and Co., Glasgow (Yard No.119).
17.11.1871: Registered at Glasgow in the ownership of Thomas Skinner and Co., Glasgow as GORDON CASTLE.
18.11.1871: Completed.
1887: Sold to Neil McLean and Co., Glasgow.
2.6.1897: Sold by court order at Cape Town to C.H. Knight and A. Cunningham of Cape Town. Re-registered at Cape Town.
22.6.1897: J.R.H. Thomson of London commissioned to sell the vessel in Glasgow for not less than £2,500.
30.9.1897: Sold to T.W. McIntyre, Glasgow.
5.10.1897: Transferred back to Glasgow registry.
17.12.1897: Sold to Steamship 'Gordon Castle' Co. Ltd. (Maclay and McIntyre, managers), Glasgow.
10.9.1900: Sank after collision with the German steamship STORMARN (Nord-Ostsee Rederi, Hamburg, 588/1880) in Cardigan Bay whilst on a voyage from Benisaf to Barrow with a cargo of iron ore. 18 crew and 1 passenger lost.
3.10.1900: Register closed.

18. DRUMMOND CASTLE 1872-1873 Iron steamer.

O.N. 63877 1,985g 1,350n 307.9 x 34.3 x 25.4 feet.
C.2-cyl. by J. and G. Thomson and Co., Glasgow; 255 NHP.
28.12.1871: Launched by J. and G. Thomson and Co., Glasgow (Yard No.120).
15.3.1872: Registered at Glasgow in the name of Thomas Skinner and Co.
18.3.1872: Completed.
31.5.1873: Wrecked on Chinsan Island whilst on a voyage from Hankow to London. All saved.
5.8.1873: Register closed.

19. BRAEMAR CASTLE 1873-1880 Iron steamer.

O.N. 68029 2,182g 1,425n 325.2 x 35.3 x 26.3 feet.
C. 2-cyl. by J. and G. Thomson and Co., Clydebank; 300 NHP.
14.2.1873: Launched by J. and G. Thomson and Co., Clydebank (Yard No. 125).
12.5.1873: Registered at Glasgow in the name of Thomas Skinner and Co., Glasgow and London.
17.5.1873: Completed.
29.10.1880: Run down at night by the British steamer BRECONSHIRE (1,800/1878) while at anchor in Penang harbour whilst on a voyage from London to Penang, Singapore, Hong Kong, Shanghai, Yokohama and Hiago. Sank in deep water under tow. All saved. Cargo partially salved.
14.3.1881: Register closed.

20. CAWDOR CASTLE 1873-1876 Iron steamer.

O.N. 68033 2,173g 1,420n 325.0 x 35.3 x 26.3 feet.
C. 2-cyl. by J. and G. Thomson and Co., Clydebank; 300 NHP.
13.5.1873: Launched by J. and G. Thomson and Co., Clydebank (Yard No. 126).
14.7.1873: Registered at Glasgow in the name of Thomas Skinner and Co., London.
15.7.1873: Completed.
7.10.1876: Wrecked at Kedgeree in the Hooghly whilst proceeding down river in charge of a pilot on a voyage from Calcutta to Colombo. Three members of the European and five of the Chinese crew drowned.
14.12.1876: Register closed.

21. GLAMIS CASTLE 1874-1887 Iron steamer.

O.N. 68099 2,340g 1,529n 331.9 x 35.7 x 26.4 feet.
C. 2-cyl. by Rait and Lindsay, Glasgow; 300 NHP.
1888: T.3-cyl. by Barclay Curle and Co. Ltd., Glasgow.
20.2.1874: Launched by Aitken and Mansel, Whiteinch, Glasgow.
7.5.1874: Registered at Glasgow in the name of Thomas Skinner and Co., London.
18.7.1887: Sold to Donaldson Brothers, Glasgow.
19.4.1888: Old register closed and re-named and re-registered at Glasgow as CIRCE in the names of John Donaldson (38/64), Archibald Falconer Donaldson (20/64), Alexander McBride (4/64) and John Blair (2/64).

1888: Re-engined by Barclay Curle and Co. Ltd., Glasgow.
18.7.1891: Wrecked on East Cape, Anticosti Island, Gulf of St. Lawrence with the loss of five lives, whilst on a voyage from Glasgow to Montreal with general cargo.
12.8.1891: Register closed.

22. FLEURS CASTLE 1874-1882 Iron steamer.

O.N. 71671 2,472g 1,622n 326.0 x 35.4 x 27.4 feet.
C .2-cyl. by J. and G. Thomson and Co., Clydebank; 300 NHP, 1,275 IHP, 11.5 knots.
27.8.1874: Launched by J. and G. Thomson and Co., Clydebank (Yard No. 132).
20.7.1874: Registered at Glasgow in the name of Thomas Skinner and Co., London.
28.10.1874: Completed.
9.7.1882: Wrecked at Ras Asir, near Cape Guardafui whilst on a voyage from Hankow to London. 27 lost. 18 survivors rescued by Holt's ANTENOR several weeks later and landed at Aden.
18.8.1882: Register closed.

23. DUNNOTTAR CASTLE 1875-1886 Iron ship.

O.N. 71692 1,750g 1,702n 258.2 x 38.6 x 23.5 feet.
24.12.1874: Launched by J. and G. Thomson and Co., Clydebank (Yard No. 135).
22.1.1875: Registered at Glasgow in the name of Thomas Skinner and Co., London.
27.1.1875: Completed.
15.7.1886: Wrecked off Cure Island, North Pacific whilst on a voyage from Sydney, New South Wales to Wilmington, California with a cargo of coal.
29.12.1886: Register closed.

24. CULZEAN CASTLE 1875 Iron ship.

O.N. 71705 1,818g 1,775n 259.3 x 40.5 x 23.0 feet.
23.2.1875: Launched by Thomas Wingate and Co., Whiteinch (Yard No. 186).
16.3.1875: Registered at Glasgow in the name of Thomas Skinner and Co., London.
25.5.1875: Sailed from Liverpool on a voyage to Melbourne, last sighted on 29.6.1875, disappeared.
15.12.1875: Posted missing.
2.3.1876: Register closed.

25. BRODICK CASTLE 1875-1886 Iron ship.

O.N. 71743. 1,827g. 1,785n. 258.6 x 40.3 x 23.0 feet.
22.6.1875: Launched by Thomas Wingate and Co., Whiteinch (Yard No.187).
30.7.1875: Registered at Glasgow in names of Thomas Skinner, Archibald Arrol and William Birrell.
31.12.1886: Re-registered at Glasgow in name of John Black and Co.
4.1.1904: Sold to Ship Brodick Castle Co. Ltd. (Hind, Rolph and Co, managers), Victoria, British Columbia and re-registered at Victoria.
6.12.1908: Sailed from Astoria, Oregon for the United Kingdom and disappeared.
31.12.1909: Register closed.

26. LOUDON CASTLE (2) 1877-1887 Iron steamer.

O.N. 76721 2,472g 1,616n 350.7 x 36.8 x 25.7 feet.
C. 2-cyl. by J. and G. Thomson and Co., Clydebank; 400 NHP, 2,790 IHP, 13.5 knots.
1897: T. 3-cyl. by C. and T.T. Pattison, Naples; 228 NHP.
19.10.1876: Launched by J. and G. Thomson and Co., Clydebank (Yard No.146).
30.12.1876: Registered at Glasgow in the name of Thomas Skinner and Co., London.
13.1.1877: Completed.
19.1.1887: Glasgow register closed. Re-registered at London.
1.1887: Sold to Nav. Gen. Italiana and renamed MARCO MINGHETTI.
20.1.1887: Register closed.
1897: New engines fitted by C. and T.T. Pattison, Naples.
1910: Sold to Soc. Nazionale di Servizi Marittimi.
1913: Sold to Sicilia Societa di Navigazione, Palermo.
1923: Broken up.

27. KENMURE CASTLE 1879-1883 Iron steamer.

O.N. 65479 1,951g 1,269n 286.0 x 35.2 x 24.9 feet.
C. 2-cyl. by Hawks, Crosby and Co., Glasgow; 200 NHP.
12.1873: Launched by J. Softley and Co., South Shields.
19.2.1874: Registered at North Shields in the ownership of Thomas Sutton as BURMESE.
1879: Acquired by Thomas Skinner and Co., London.
13.11.1879: Renamed KENMURE CASTLE and re-registered at London in the name of Thomas Skinner and Co.
2.2.1883: Foundered in a storm in the Bay of Biscay. 32 lost, 16 saved.
10.3.1883: Register closed.

28. BOTHWELL CASTLE (2) 1881-1896 Iron steamer.

O.N. 82872 2,542g 1,653n 319.1 x 38.0 x 28.0 feet.
C. 2-cyl. Thomas Richardson and Sons, Hartlepool; 300 NHP.
3.1881: Launched by R. Dixon and Co., Middlesbrough (Yard No. 180).
25.4.1881: Registered at London in the name of Thomas Skinner and Co.

6.3.1882: Transferred to Bothwell Castle Steamship Owners Ltd. (Thomas Skinner and Co., managers), London.
1.2.1892: Transferred to Bothwell Castle Steamship Owners Ltd. (1889) (T. Skinner and Co., managers), London.
4.1892: 18/64 shares sold to McIlwraith and McEacharn and Co. Ltd, London and Melbourne. Management shared between Skinner and new owners.
22.2.1895: J.C. and G.R. Stewart, solicitors, Melbourne, commissioned to sell vessel for not less than £9,000.
12.1.1896: Sold outright to McIlwraith and McEacharn and Co., London and Melbourne.
9.10.1896: London registry closed.
17.11.1896: Re-registered at Melbourne.
21.2.1899: Renamed COOLGARDIE.
23.12.1913: Sold to W. Crosby and Co., Melbourne.
22.3.1916: Sold to James Wardle and Co., Melbourne.
2.11.1917: James Wardle died, willing vessel to F.A. Verco, Melbourne.
10.1.1920: Sold to Eastern Shipping Agencies Ltd., Melbourne.
1922: Sold by court order at Marseilles. Broken up in Italy.

The *Bothwell Castle* is seen, above, in Skinner's ownership, and below in later life as McIlwraith and McEacharn's *Coolgardie.* Comparison of the photographs, and that on page 254, shows that she lost the yards on the foremast and gained a narrower funnel, with what is possibly a donkey boiler funnel. *[Above: National Maritime Museum S8/777; Below: Ian Farquhar collection]*

A ship so good they named her twice: in Italian ownership the *Nord America* continues to display her original name *Stirling Castle*. [World Ship Photo Library collection]

29. STIRLING CASTLE 1882-1883. Iron steamer.
O.N. 85108 4,423g 2,004n 418.6 x 50.0 x 30.8 feet.
C. 2-cyl. by J. Elder and Co., Glasgow; 1,500 NHP.
21.1.1882: Launched by J. Elder and Co., Glasgow (Yard No. 257).
28.2.1882: Registered at London in the name of Thomas Skinner and Co.
14.8.1882: Transferred to Stirling Castle Steamship Owners Ltd. (T. Skinner and Co., managers), London
10.1883: Sold to M. Bruzzo and Co., Genoa, Italy and renamed NORD AMERICA.
20.10.1883: Register closed.
1884: Owner became La Veloce Linea di Navigazone a Vapore, Genoa.
4.1885: Sold to J.W. Adamson (Adamson and Ronaldson, managers), London and renamed STIRLING CASTLE.
21.4.1885: Chartered to British Government as a troopship at 23s. per ton.
28.4.1885: Re-registered at Malta in the ownership of James Wilkie Adamson.
20.10.1885: Returned to owners. Total hire paid £36,870.

12.1.1886: Re-sold to Italian owners and reverted to NORD AMERICA. Malta register closed.
1888: Owner became La Veloce Linea di Navigazione a Vapore S.A., Genoa.
1900: Re-built and fitted with triple expansion engines.
1909: Reduced to cargo only.
6.12.1910: Stranded near Cape Spartel whilst on a voyage from Buenos Aires to Genoa with a cargo of horses. Refloated and towed to Genoa.
1911: Broken up at Genoa.

30. MINARD CASTLE 1882-1883 Iron steamer.
O.N. 85115 2,460g 1,596n 322.0 x 38.3 x 26.0 feet.
C. 2-cyl. by Thomas Richardson and Sons, Hartlepool; 350 NHP.
12.1881: Launched by R. Dixon and Co., Middlesbrough.
3.1882: Completed.
23.3.1882: Registered at London in the name of Thomas Skinner and Co.
14.8.1882: Transferred to Minard Castle Steamship Owners Ltd. (T. Skinner and Co., managers), London.
10.4.1883: Sank after striking a submerged rock off Chungchow Island on a voyage from Hong Kong to Saigon. All saved.
25.6.1883: Register closed.

SOURCES AND ACKNOWLEDGEMENTS
Photographs are from the collection of John Clarkson unless otherwise credited. We thank all who gave permission for their photographs to be used, and for help in finding photographs we are particularly grateful to Tony Smith, Jim McFaul and David Whiteside of the World Ship Photo Library; to Ian Farquhar, Fred Hawks, Bill Laxon, Peter Newall, Ivor Rooke, William Schell, George Scott; to David Hodge and Bob Todd of the National Maritime Museum; Dr. David Jenkins of the National Museums and Galleries of Wales; and other museums and institutions listed.
Research sources have included the *Registers* of William Schell and Tony Starke, *Lloyd's Register, Lloyd's Confidential Index, Lloyd's War Losses, Mercantile Navy Lists,* and *Marine News.* Use of the facilities of the World Ship Society's Central Record, the Guildhall Library, the Public Record Office and Lloyd's Register of Shipping are gratefully acknowledged. Particular thanks also to William Schell and John Bartlett for various information, to Heather Fenton for editorial and indexing work, and to Marion Clarkson for accountancy services.

Thomas Skinner's Castle Line
Public Record Office: BT31 wound up company files; BT108 closed registers, Glasgow and London; BT109 closed register transactions.
Merseyside Maritime Museum - Glen Line papers.
Glasgow University Business Archives - John Brown papers.
N.R.P Bonsor, *North Atlantic Seaway* T. Stephenson: London, 1955 and *South Atlantic Seaway* Brookside, Jersey, 1983.

A.G. Davies 'Thomas Skinner and Co., Glasgow' *Sea Breezes* Vol.17 (1933) pages 208-9.
Basil Lubbock, *The Last of the Windjammers Vol. I* Brown, Son and Ferguson, Glasgow, 1927.
Basil Lubbock, *The China Clippers* James Brown and Son, Glasgow, 1914.
David MacGregor, *The Tea Clippers,* rev.ed. Conway Maritime Press, London, 1983.
Thanks also to Tom Stevens for his notes on *Bothwell Castle* and his extracts from the McIlwraith papers held at the Australian National University, Canberra, and to Bill Laxon for his notes on the fleet list.

Shaw, Savill's Big Ics
David Aitchison, *Royal Standard, Red Ensign.* Pall Mall Press, London, 1958.
Richard de Kerbrech, *Shaw, Savill and Albion; The Post-War Fortunes of a Shipping Empire.* Conway, London, 1986.
Andrew Bell, 'Shaw Savill's Corinthic Class'. *Ships Monthly,* August 2000.
Shipbuilder and Marine Engine Builder, July 1947

Garston
J.M. Tolson, *The St. Helens Railway - its Rivals and Successor* Oakwood Press, 1982.
Duncan Haws, *Merchant Fleets - Elders & Fyffes and Geest.* TCL Publications, Uckfield, 1996.

PUTTING THE RECORD STRAIGHT

Letters, additions, amendments and photographs relating to articles in any issues of *Record* are welcomed. Letters may be lightly edited. E-mails are welcome, but senders are asked to include their postal address.

Eastern Dry Dock

I read with interest in *Record 22* the article on Turner, Brightman. My eye was caught by the photograph of *Zarate* in dry dock in 1888 and David Hodge's doubts about its whereabouts. From 1939 to 1943 I was an apprentice with Mountstuart Dry Docks Ltd. and most of that time was spent at the Eastern Dry Dock on the eastern bank of the River Usk at Newport. There is no doubt in my mind that this is a photograph of the Eastern Dry Dock. The row of cottages were still there when I left to join the Merchant Navy. Alongside the Eastern Dry Dock was the Channel Dry Dock also operated by Mountstuart, as was the Tredegar Dry Dock on the town side of the River Usk.

I visited the site last week after 60 years and found that Eastern Dry Dock is now operated by RMC Aggregates and the dock itself is the berth for a Bristol Channel sand dredger. The lock gate has gone and the wooden jetties are rotting away and falling into the river. I had a conversation with Mike Daly, the Depot Foreman, and showed him the photo. He confirmed that, when he first started there in the 1960s, the row of cottages still existed but have now disappeared under an industrial estate. The Channel Dry Dock is now operated by Bird Port as a container terminal; until recently it was used by Bell Lines and as a general cargo dock.
PHILIP WOOD, Brockwells Cottage, Caerwent, Caldicot, Monmouthshire NP26 5AS
Other correspondence on Turner, Brightman has been held over: see Introduction. Ed.

More on ore

Thank you once again for a very interesting issue of *Record,* with excellent photographs of the vessels. With regard to the photograph of *Orecrest* (page 165, top) with the crest on the bow, I have looked at it with a magnifying glass and, as a professor of Classics, I'm fairly certain that there is only one possibility, namely the Latin word LIBERTAS, rendered LI/BER/TAS, meaning of course 'freedom'. Why Crest Shipping might have chosen this motto I have no idea.
VIC MATTHEWS, 9 Maple Street, Guelph, Ontario, Canada, N1G 2G3

I greatly enjoyed the article on the iron ore ships - most useful. I am intrigued as to why the Welsh owners (with the exception of Gibbs) at the time steered clear of the business, especially as it was money easily made!

Just for the record, the view of *Redcar* on page156 is approaching the Queen Alexandra Lock, Cardiff, that of *Paxo* (this ship was presumably stuffed, not loaded!) on page 160 is in the Queen Alexandra Dock, that of *Queensgarth* on page 164 is also in the Queen Alexandra Dock, with the funnels of either *Bristol Queen* or *Cardiff Queen* visible behind, and that of *Orecrest* on page 165 is entering the Queen Alexandra Lock.
Dr DAVID JENKINS, National Museums and Galleries of Wales, Heol Crochendy, Parc Nantgarw CF15 7QT

I found John Harrison's piece about the Iron Ladies in *Record 23* of great interest. I enclose a photograph of the *Dapo Sailor* (ex-*Monksgarth*) at the Bidston Dock iron ore terminal, Birkenhead, on 26th February 1978 (below). She had been discharging iron ore from Puerto Ordaz, Venezuela which was destined for the Shotton steelworks in North Wales. She was due to return to Birkenhead on 18th March that year with another consignment, this time from Nouadhibou, Mauritania. She was a regular trader to Birkenhead as the *Monksgarth,* and continued to trade there under the Greek flag. Her funnel markings are those of Armenakis Brothers, although the Dapo in her name was inspired by owners E. Pothitos and N.A. Davaris.

The three grabbing appliances, which were once a landmark at Birkenhead, were dismantled in the latter part of 1992. Bidston also had a steel mill, but that was dismantled about 1990, and shipped for re-use in China.
PETER MYERS, 69 Westbank Park, Old Meldrum, Inverurie, Aberdeenshire AB51 0DG

Tweaks to 23

Two minor points in *Record 23.* Page 156, third and fourth lines in left column: 'GD' is not part of the builder's name, but rather abbreviation of part of the place name - Grand Quevilly.
Page 182, Arndt is correct. However, *Sperrbrecher 14* was a different *Bockenheim,* the former Wilhelmsen *Tai Ping* (7,019/1929) caught in Norway in April 1940.
WILLIAM SCHELL, 334 So. Franklin Street, Holbrook, MA 02343, USA

INDEX TO RECORD 21 TO 24

Record 21: pp.1-64; *Record 22:* 65-128; *Record 23:* pp.129-192; *Record 24:* 193-264.

Index of articles

Index of ships

Gothic at Cape Town in royal yacht colours (see page 200). *[World Ship Photo Library collection]*